Making Britain Literate

Kevin Norley

Imprimata

Published by **Imprimata**
Copyright © Kevin Norley 2009, 2012

2nd Edition 2012

Every effort has been made to seek permission to re-produce
various articles that appear in this publication. The publisher will
be pleased to correct any errors or ommisions for future editions.

A CIP Catalogue record for this book is available
from the British Library

ISBN 978-1-906192-67-9

Printed in Great Britain

Imprimata

An imprint of InXmedia Limited
www.imprimata.co.uk

Reviews for Kevin Norley's books

'I found *Making Britain Literate* an excellent, comprehensive and thought-provoking book. Crucially, it should be an extremely effective tool and a remedy for all kinds of entrenched malaise within our educational system. And it manages to combine rigour with accessibility and fun. It deserves great praise.'

Lee M, The Plain English Campaign

'*Making Britain Literate* and *Making Britain Numerate*... cover key requirements for teaching basic literacy and numeracy. Suitable for professional teachers and homeschoolers, both books include helpful examples and exercises.'

Newsletter No 70, Spring 2010, Campaign for Real Education

'I recently passed both my L2 literacy and numeracy at Bedford College. I found the ideas contained in both Mr Norley's books really useful. I developed a better understanding of English (which is my second language), particularly with the grammar, which even helped me with my maths.'

Marilyn L (Bedford College, June 2010)

'(*Making Britain Numerate*) is a superb book which can be used as a study guide for anyone wishing to improve their own numeracy skills, or help someone else with theirs. I have used it with many of my staff and all have commented at how easy it is to grasp the concepts within it. All have shown improvements in their numeracy skills.'

Steve W, Area Manager, VT Training, East of England, March 2009, Amazon.co.uk

'I have recently finished a maths course at the Luton Learning Centre. There were 15 of us on the course, from all different parts of the world. Kevin showed us very clearly how to work with fractions and percentages, how to convert from one to the other, and how those conversions can be used to both better understand and solve problems including those involving scale and volume. His explanations were detailed, and he had high expectations of all of us. Needless to say, I achieved my L2 numeracy qualification.'

Caroline O (Luton Learning Centre, July '10)

'I needed a level 2 numeracy qualification in order to be accepted onto a BSc Social Work and Mental Health Nursing degree course, so I attended a numeracy workshop at the Skillsbank. The resources used and methods taught from '*Making Britain Numerate*' were very straightforward and ideal for ensuring that I obtained my qualification quickly!'

Charity M (Bedford College, June '10)

'The level 3 numeracy staff training carried out by Mr Norley was based on a range of strategies that built on clear and precise methods, all of which are detailed in his book, *Making Britain Numerate*. All the group passed their level 3 application of number test."

Kevin G, Internal Verifier - Training, Babcock International Group

'One of the things I find interesting about *Making Britain Literate*, is that it attempts to address both the literacy and language needs of native speakers and ESOL students in one book. It values, for example, the importance of the understanding of grammar and word classes in developing literacy and language skills.'

Michael M, English Language Tutor, Challney Community College, Luton

Functional Skills: essential resources

Making Britain Numerate (2nd Ed) and Making Britain Literate (2nd Ed) are two workbooks written to support learners (including ESOL learners) studying Functional Skills either as part of an apprenticeship or as stand-alone qualifications.

The books contain a detailed analysis of the main issues surrounding the development of learners' literacy, language and numeracy skills as well as a wide range of ideas, methods and up-to-date contextualised materials. The resources offer worked examples and a step by step guide through all areas required for achievement of functional skills maths and English (including numerous reading, writing, discussion and presentation exercises).

Campaign for Learning E-Newsletter, May 17th 2012

For further reviews, go to
www.skillsforlifenetwork.com/making-britain-numerate-literate

I would like to dedicate this book
to my mother and to my wife.

How is English used today?

"I done it before. I rit it there!" exclaimed Sarah, her softly spoken voice raising a pitch and taking me back slightly, but not enough to stall my retort, as I had anticipated it.

"Uh I think you mean 'I did it before. I wrote it there'" I said calmly, smiling. Sensing no adverse reaction, I continued.

"Just tell me something, Sarah. You recently spent 11 years in state schools from 5 – 16, right."

"uh huh"

"During that time, did anyone at your school or in your home environment, or anyone for that matter, correct your English?"

"Maybe… I don't know… I guess not." she replied with a nervous smile.

"That's o.k." I said. "Don't worry about it. I mean many people in our society speak the same way" I continued, in a rather apologetic tone. "It's not a big deal". I wanted to be quick to play it down, not to make her feel bad in any way.

Sarah was in a way the ideal person to 'experiment' on, to prove to myself what I already knew. She was one of the brighter learners in the class, quiet and good natured. She was coming to the end of her 8 week short intensive basic skills programme, one of the programmes designed for unemployed people sent to the training organisation I worked for by the job centre to improve her literacy and numeracy skills. She'd progressed well with her level 1 adult literacy and numeracy, and would take her L1 tests soon and move on. The environment was ideal too. A small class of unemployed adults, individuals, each with their own difficulties in life, their own issues, but no group mentality, generally passive and subdued. What's more, they were used to my social class foibles, reminding them to pronounce their 't's, 'th's and 'h's, to say you 'were' not you 'was', not to use double negatives etc. They were also used to me nagging them about the importance of reading as much as possible in order to improve their literacy and increase their everyday vocabulary.

How was I able to get away with this? Well, for a while I was their teacher, and having built up a good relationship with the students, I could get away with trying. It wasn't easy though, nor was I successful 'Why does it matter how I speak?' 'That's how my mum speaks', 'Everyone else speaks like this', 'I don't want to talk posh'. I was familiar with that one, and would often counter that there weren't just two ways of speaking i.e. 'street language' and 'posh', that there was plain 'ole standard English too, although not to much avail, as I was aware that this was often perceived as 'posh' too. It was difficult to win an argument or convince anyone of the need to speak standard English, or what I was trying to portray as 'correct' grammar and pronunciation, and they must have wondered why I bothered. I would emphasise however that I believed that people should feel free to express themselves the way they want to, but that at the same time they needed to know how and when to use standard English. I didn't expect them to 'talk posh' when they were having a drink with their friends, but I expected them to know, in an educational or professional environment, how to utilise standard English for their own advantage.

I would also emphasise that the way in which any member of a social group converses, and the pronunciation they use, will depend upon the situation they're in. The variety of language then that any member uses that is appropriate for that particular situation is known as a *register*. For example, when doctors explain problems to patients, they try to avoid the medical, specialised terms, so that they can make themselves understood. However, the same ideas will be conveyed in a different, more technical language when those doctors are discussing the cases with their colleagues. Another example could be the language used by TV presenters. During broadcasting they are likely to use standard English and received pronunciation (RP). However, the same people will speak in a different way while having a drink with their friends, or while playing with their children. These examples then serve to illustrate the relationship between contextual language and social group.

The English language has been subject to a multitude of influences over the years, and has inevitably changed with time. There has been much written about how, and the extent to which language has evolved over time, and the main influences on the language (e.g. Knowles 1997, Hughes and Trudgill 1979). It would be fair then to say that language use within any of the social groups that make up the English speaking population has changed over the years, and is therefore not fixed. However, I would argue that language use itself is determined by the social groups in which we live, and that although it changes, differences remain between the language use of those social groups, and that those differences in language use in turn, determine the the social group we belong to. This fact is highlighted by Kramsch (1998: 3) for example, who explains that 'members of a... social group do not only express experience; they also create experience through language', and goes on to argue that:

> The way in which people use the spoken, written, or visual medium itself creates meanings that are understandable to the group they belong to ...
>
> **(Kramsch 1998: 3)**

In terms of the social groups themselves, Gardiner (2003) states that:

> Examples of social groups that might be said to have their own distinctive styles of language use include those based on socio-economic status, age, occupation and gender.'
>
> **(Gardiner 2003:32)**

There has been a lot of research into the extent to which language use is affected by which social group one belongs to. Gardiner (2003: 33) outlines briefly the effects of the above-mentioned social groups on language use when, for example, he writes about how some occupations have their ''own specialist vocabulary' or 'jargon', how women and men 'use language in different ways' and how speech differs between 'teenagers' and 'older members of the same community.'

This specialist vocabulary can be said to reinforce a profession or trade's identity and help its members to communicate with greater clarity, economy and precision. The legal, medical, IT and teaching professions are examples of professions that use quite specialist vocabulary. Using specialist vocabulary can however give the users a feeling of self importance and serve to exclude people from outside a particular profession or trade. In terms of gender, it has been found that women's accents are less pronounced and that their language generally tends more towards standard English than men's. Also, research has shown that men are more assertive and less co-operative than women in conversational interaction. This can be demonstrated through observing how men 'butt in' more often during conversations, and swear more often (Eames and Wainwright 1999). In terms of age, teenagers and young people in general have a large and ever changing lexicon of slang words and colloquialisms which strengthen their identity as a social group. Knowles (1997: 5) makes an analogy between young people adopting 'new styles of speech' and 'new styles of dress and other social habits.' Furthermore, people of all generations often stick with the informal lexis of their youth e.g. popular words with young people in the sixties included 'pad', 'chick' and 'pot', whilst in the nineties they included 'eco-warriors', 'surfing the net' and 'spin-doctor.'

Socio-economic status shall be looked at shortly, but going back to my students, I appreciated the fact that if they had left school and were speaking with such grammar, there wasn't a lot that I could do, in effective isolation and in a short period of time. I was also aware that this was just one of many examples of how the argument for the importance and relevance for the use of standard spoken English had been lost. I would show newspaper articles on the importance of the spoken word, how employers decry the slovenly decline of the spoken word amongst the youth, and how it affects their job opportunities etc. I would be careful to portray it as 'just someone else's view and move on quickly. I was aware that the reasons these guys didn't work went well beyond the way they spoke. I was just trying to illustrate it as a factor.

Wind forward a few years. I was attending a 3 day teachers' conference entitled 'Teaching the Teacher Trainer' in which the main focus was the delivery of new teaching qualifications (Preparing to Teach in the Lifelong Learning Sector (PTLLS), Certificate in Teaching in the Lifelong Learning Sector (CTLLS) and the Diploma in Teaching in the Lifelong Learning Sector (DTLLS)) in relation to new standards. The conference included several useful workshops such as, 'The role of the teacher educator', 'Approaches to teaching and learning',

'Reflective practice' and 'Principles of effective feedback'. As part of one the workshops, we were split into groups of 5, and given the task of preparing a short (15 minute) presentation reflecting on how we would deliver an element of the new standards for the literacy and/or ESOL subject specialisms for the DTLLS. My chosen element was an analysis of the personal, social and cultural factors influencing literacy learners' development of spoken and written language. Within this area then, I chose to focus on the teaching and learning of grammar in relation to social class, and in the context of, developing speaking and listening, and writing skills, of adult learners.

So, I began my presentation by outlining my objectives along with some supportive theory upon which I was to base some of my arguments. The plan was then to outline, based on my experience, and with practical examples, why I felt the teaching of Standard English through constant and consistent error correction of grammar and pronunciation was important in improving learners' speaking and listening skills and how doing so would give them a wider base upon which to develop other literacy skills. This was to be done in the context of acknowledging the potential difficulties and awkwardness of correcting adults' speech and subtle ways in which this could be addressed. With this in mind, the argument was to be set against what I believe to be the prevailing orthodoxy in many educational environments relating to spoken grammar and pronunciation i.e. to accept equally all forms of spoken grammatical variations related to socio-economic group and region. Following this, the arguments were to be opened up for discussion.

Leading on from my introduction, I highlighted the afore-mentioned comment, 'I done it before. I rit it there', as an example of the common use of non-standard English which in my opinion should have been anticipated and not allowed to develop within the eleven years of a pupil's educational experience but which should still nevertheless be corrected if used as an adult (or post-16) learner. Within the time limitation that I had, I didn't plan to discuss or even touch upon pronunciation. The general trend was that while someone was presenting, the others would listen, and only interrupt to seek clarification or supplement the presentation with a supporting comment or anecdote. However, maybe due to the nature of my presentation, this was to change. Following on from my analysis, I was interrupted by one of the course's facilitators with a comment of, 'To me that is standard English'. This provoked a response from me seeking clarification on the comment, which in turn led to a range of views from the group which were broadly critical of the stance I had, till then, been taking. The discussion became slightly heated. Off script, I gave examples of how I thought, generally speaking, that in work environments, one could relate the level of a person's occupation to the way they spoke (i.e. their grammar and pronunciation), which led to another critical comment. I managed to get back on to my presentation and hurried through the remainder of it, although indeed an uncomfortable atmosphere had been created.

In terms of socio-economic status, or social class, there has been much written about the correlation between language use and educational attainment and culture, a lot of which has been the subject of some quite contentious debate. Much of the issue has surrounded the use of 'standard English' and 'non-standard English' dialects, and whether or not the former is 'better' or 'superior' to the latter, and accent variations (the use of 'Received Pronunciation' (RP) as compared with regional non-RP accents). The grammatical and lexical (vocabulary) differences between non-standard British dialects and standard English, along with comparisons between RP and regional non-RP accents are outlined in detail by Hughes and Trudgill (1979) in their study of social and regional varieties of British English. In their study, they define the term 'standard English' as 'the dialect of educated people throughout the British Isles' (1979: 8). Trudgill (1994: 6) puts forward a clear argument that the use of non-standard dialects is, '… not 'wrong' in any way… ' and that the use of non-standard forms:

> '… should not be regarded as 'mistakes'. They are used by millions of English speakers around the world and are representative of grammatical systems that are different from Standard English, not linguistically inferior to it.'
>
> **(Trudgill 1994: 6)**

In contrast to this, Honey (1997) in his book 'Language is Power', argues that schools have been failing working-class and ethnic minority children through not insisting on the exclusive use of standard English, and states that:

> '… to give access to standard English to those members of society who have not acquired facility in it through their parents, is an important priority in any society concerned with social justice and the reduction of educational inequalities.'
>
> **(Honey 1997: 5)**

When considered alongside a claim from Clark and Ivanic (1997: 55) that schools' literacy policies exclude 'powerless social groups… from contributing to the collective store of knowledge, cultural and ideological activity', then it becomes clear just how contentious and important the issue can be.

Entwhistle (1978: 32), in emphasising the differences between the social classes in terms of their different cultures and associated linguistic differences, explains the difficulties that working-class children have traditionally had in schooling as being partly due to 'the inability of working-class speech to support academic discourse'. Furthermore, Bernstein (1964: 25), in studying social relationships and how they tend to generate different speech systems (or linguistic codes), argued that the failure of children from working-class origins to profit from formal education was 'crudely related to the control on types of learning induced by a restricted code'. In outlining the difference between what he defines as 'elaborated' and 'restricted' codes in terms of class structures, he states that:

> … children socialised within middle class and associated strata can be expected to possess both an elaborated and a restricted code whilst children socialised within some sections of the working class strata, particularly the lower working class, can be expected to be limited to a restricted code. As a child progresses through school it becomes critical for him to possess, or at least to be oriented towards, an elaborated code, if he is to succeed.
>
> **(Bernstein 1964: 5)**

There have been a variety of cases whereby parents, including politicians, whilst supporting the principle of comprehensive schools, have sent their own children to private, independent or grammar schools. The reasons behind this apparent contradiction cannot necessarily be ascertained. Whilst it is natural to want the best for one's children, what can be difficult to fathom, is why measures which would enhance children's spoken language skills (such as the insistence on the use of Standard English) cannot be implemented and supported, such that many more can achieve within comprehensive schools. An interesting anecdote relating to the above came during the interview for a magazine article, conducted by Brown (2008) in the 'Sunday Telegraph', of a well known musician to commemorate his 50th birthday. In the interview, the musician, who had been involved during the 80s in many Labour Party causes, said in relation to why he sent his children to private schools, that he didn't want them, '… coming home speaking like Ali G …'

However, it should be made clear here that the idea of the failure of working-class children being related to linguistic, or cultural deprivation has been challenged by several linguists, including Labov (1972: 201) who, in his studies in the use of black English vernacular of children in urban ghettos, argued that 'the concept of verbal deprivation has no basis in social reality'. Furthermore, Cameron, in her book 'Verbal Hygiene' has argued that:

> 'Non-standard and unconventional uses of language can only be seen as a threat to communication if communication itself is conceived in a way that negates our whole experience of it.'
>
> **(Cameron 1995: 25)**

More recent research, reported by Clark (2009: 1) in the 'Daily Mail' has found that many children from socio-economically disadvantaged backgrounds start school unable to speak or communicate properly as a result of being brought up in environments where there is a lack of communication, and that their speech and language skills are well below children of a similar age.

During the summer of 2008 there was a fiasco relating to the production of the key stage SATS (Standard Attainment Targets) results within schools across England. The fiasco centred around both the late production of many of the results and the many complaints related to the accuracy of the marking. One of the many cases that was highlighted concerned the marking of two key stage 2 English papers for 11 year olds at a school in England. It was reported in newspapers that the primary school head had complained about the marking on the basis that the 2 papers (written by pupil A and pupil B) had been scored equally for sentence structure (5 out of 8 for each) and that pupil B had scored one mark more for composition and effect (9 out of 10 compared with 8 out of 10). Sections of the papers in question were as follows:

Pupil A
Quickly, it became apparent that Pip was a fantastic rider: a complete natural. But it was his love of horses that led to a tragic accident. An accident that would change his life forever. At the age of 7, he was training for...

Pupil B
If he wasent doing enth'ing els heel help his uncle Herry at the funfair during the day. And then hed stoody at nigh...

Although the assessment clearly calls into question how such markers were recruited by the QCA (DfES) to assess the key stage 2 English papers and to what extent they were qualified and trained for the job, it also begs the question as to what extent, and how quickly, pupils who make such errors in their writing assessments are given the opportunity to learn from their mistakes and develop their literacy skills as they progress through compulsory education. Furthermore, on the basis that such errors are commonplace amongst pupils, and always have been, it begs the question as to what extent could they be anticipated and measures put into place to ensure learning through consistent reinforcement of correct spelling, grammar and punctuation across all academic subject areas. Alongside these questions, I also reflect on the extent to which pupils pass through the education system without having their spoken language, in terms of their grammar and pronunciation constantly and consistently corrected where necessary.

At the time of writing (2009), a well rehearsed presentation is going around the schools and colleges of the country highlighting radical changes that are occurring within the 14 – 19 national curriculum, including changes to GCSEs, the introduction of functional skills, the introduction of new foundation, higher and advanced diplomas, an increase in the number and range of apprenticeships, an employment with training option at 16 and the introduction of a Foundation Learning Tier for those learners not ready for a full level 2 qualification. During the video clips within the presentation, school and college managers, teachers and students alike reflect positively on the new qualifications and the range of options available at 14, 16, 17 and 18. What was not reflected on during the presentation however, was how those students studying within the Foundation Learning Tier spoke with non-standard English features (with regard to their pronunciation and grammar) as compared with those students aiming for higher level qualifications, whose English tended more towards Standard English (with regard to their pronunciation and grammar). I raised the issue of language during questions at the end of the presentation, and related it to the absence of the speaking of Standard English from the functional skills standards. I left, as I so often do after such meetings wondering if questions I ask will ever be addressed or reflected on, whether or not such questions are ever raised by anyone elsewhere and feeling self-conscious that I may be seen at best as eccentric and at worst as a pain in the neck for having raised the subject.

At the time of writing, unions are debating whether or not to boycott SATs in England (they are not held in Wales, Scotland or Northern Ireland). The benefits of such tests to school pupils and the use to which they are put in informing school league tables are questioned in light of increased workloads for teachers and increased stress levels amongst the pupils themselves. Related to the SATS, it has also become a fairly widely held view amongst teachers that measuring is more important than learning. With this, and the above, in mind, I would propose a method of assessment whereby there is less emphasis on measuring, and more on the learning process (i.e. a learning assessment, examples of which, along with a rationale, are given later).

I should say that the situation in schools depicted earlier is clearly not uniform. The focus is on schools in areas where literacy levels amongst its pupils (and often their immediate family) is below a standard expected of their age and where the need for improved speaking skills is therefore greatest.

It should be stated however that in recent years, much money and effort have been invested by the education system in initiatives to support pupils in their literacy. Such initiatives have included the introduction in 1997 of the 'literacy hour' in the primary school curriculum and the widespread deployment of teaching assistants to support pupils with a wide range of special educational needs in primary and secondary schools. Also, even though the principle of encouraging students through praise in order to raise self esteem is one which is well established by teachers, the difficulties involved in motivating students, particularly in the context of teaching in inner-city secondary schools, can not be underestimated.

In schools where efforts have been made to improve the language of its pupils (for example in an Academy school in Manchester, where the pupils are told to use formal language (instead of street slang) with adults within the school at all times, it is regarded as a factor in the school's improved results for achievement of 5 good GCSEs.

However, as stated in the CBI report (2006: 1), *Working on the three Rs*, which was set up to explore, '… the ways in which literacy… skills are used in the workplace and the shortfalls in these skills that employers experience.':

Spelling and grammar are important and are widely seen as weak. Correct spelling of everyday words and proper use of basic grammar are important for clarity of expression and fostering a reader's confidence'

(CBI 2006: 2)

Furthermore, the report states that, '*The inability to put together a short coherent piece of writing has serious implications for those seeking work or thinking of changing jobs*'. Whilst such experiences and opinions may be commonplace amongst employers, what is not considered or reflected on in the report is why those employers do not set any literacy standard as a prerequisite for employment. If this was done, pressure could be brought to bear on whatever educational establishments the potential employees were at, or at least a dialogue established between employers and such establishments, related to expectations of the literacy levels of potential employees (taking into account however that some may have been statemented as having dyslexia or other learning disorder or disability). Behind each person with low literacy skills however is a cultural system of low expectations which allows many people to leave education and enter the work with those low literacy skills.

This low level of expectations in terms of pupils' literacy standards, which is so apparent in parts of our compulsory education system, transposes (and manifests) itself into our further education system. The whole nature of Key Skills for example does, I believe, act as a compensatory model for those students leaving school with low level literacy skills and yet reflects the low standards and low expectations of the state school system.

In my role as essential skills trainer for a private training company, I provide literacy (communication) and numeracy (application of number) tuition and support for learners who are studying for 'Skills for Life' adult literacy and numeracy qualifications and work-based learning apprenticeship and advanced apprenticeship programmes in the hospitality, retail, care and sport and leisure sectors (alongside tuition and support for the company's staff who need to achieve their level 3 key skills communication and application of number tests). The learners themselves are a mixture of males and females, of all ages (16+ although predominantly in the 16 – 21 age range), from a variety of occupations and from different regions of the country. My experience of teaching literacy to learners in my current job role (and previous job roles within further education) has clearly shown me that there is a correlation between grammar used in spoken English and the grammar used in written English, and that in some cases this is preventing learners from identifying grammatical errors in their own writing and key skills tests, and hence holding them back. Whilst tutoring learners, and facilitating 'On-Line' key skills communication and adult literacy national tests (at levels 1 and 2), I have noticed that learners make reading errors in questions relating to a knowledge of grammar, such as being aware of appropriate verb tense, subject-verb agreement, double negatives and in the use of modal verbs.

These errors may come about as a result of learners not being aware of what grammatical errors are, or when they do, not being able to recognise incorrect (or correct) grammar. Whilst a learner can be taught what grammar is (or what it relates to) and hence what grammatical errors are, it can be more difficult to teach 'correct' or 'Standard English' grammar when it contrasts with learners' spoken English, particularly if that English was not (or rarely) corrected throughout their schooling, and if that is the English they are used to speaking in their home environment

Examples of spoken 'errors' relating to appropriate verb tense include those such as:

'The players come at us' 'The players **came** at us'

'I see him in town yesterday' '**I saw** him in town yesterday'

'He run at me' 'He **ran** at me'

'They give it to him this morning' 'They **gave** it to him this morning'

Examples of spoken 'errors' relating to subject-verb agreement include:

'Was you there last night?' **'Were you …**

'It weren't really necessary' **'It wasn't** …

'We done the work earlier' **'We did …**

Examples of spoken 'errors' relating to double negatives include:

'We haven't got none' **'We haven't got any'**

'I never did nothing' '**I never did anything'**

Examples of spoken 'errors' relating to modal verbs:

'I could of have done it!' **I could have …**

'Shouldn't they of arrived this morning' **'Shouldn't they have …**

It is apparent then that written errors that learners make are a reflection on errors that learners make in their spoken English. Bearing in mind that the learners are of both genders, work in a variety of occupations, come from different regions of the country and are of different ages etc, then this, I believe is a reflection at least to a degree on the learners' socio-economic background.

Interestingly, two of the apprenticeship sector skills councils, namely 'People First' (for hospitality) and 'Sports Active' (for sport and leisure) have recently changed the required key skills attainment levels of their apprenticeship programmes, such that learners need now to obtain level one (previously level 2) in communication. Level one is regarded as equivalent to the level required by school children when they have reached the age of eleven, and is therefore a clear indication that standards are being lowered and that allowance is being made for learners' literacy and language deficit.

With regard to the Qualifications and Curriculum Authority's 'Key Skills Qualifications Standards and Guidance' (2004) it is stated that with reference to the writing of documents at any level, there should be 'a tolerance level of '… one or two spelling mistakes' and that:

> The same error occurring more than once in a single document counts as a single error. At any level, where a candidate is using punctuation, sentence structures or vocabulary beyond the demands of the standards at that level, errors in their use should not be penalised. Fitness for purpose is an important factor. Several minor errors in a document written for one's own personal use or for limited internal circulation can be considered acceptable...
>
> **(QCA 2004: 29)**

In terms of punctuation, the standards state that at level 1:

> In final work, sentences must be marked correctly by capital letters and full stops or question marks. Where other types of punctuation are used, the candidate should not be penalised for occasional errors, providing meaning is still clear.
>
> **(QCA 2004: 33)**

In other words, the use of the comma and apostrophe are not seen as important at this level. There's a strong likelihood with learners on vocational programmes that they would already have gone through a school system whereby such basics as the correct use of these punctuation marks was not given much (if any) degree of importance. To compensate for this, tutors and assessors need to mentally adjust (consciously or otherwise) by putting in their own punctuation in order to decipher meaning.

Lynne Truss's, 'Eats Shoots and Leaves' illustrates and highlights well the importance of punctuation in everyday contexts and how it can radically change meaning. However, such views relating to the importance of punctuation are criticised on the basis that its rules have exceptions and are not always clear-cut. This may be so. However, there is, I believe, a tendency for people, particularly academics, to focus on the exceptions, and I would argue that in the majority of cases of punctuation errors made by learners, the usage is simply wrong, with the required correction being both necessary and apparent. What can be difficult, is dealing with the lack of importance attached to punctuation by people in general and those in education in particular.

If we consider the fact that some assessors and teachers may not themselves have the literacy skills to identify certain grammatical, spelling and punctuation errors, combined with a broad interpretation that can be given to these standards, particularly in relation to a widely held notion that '… as long as you can still understand the meaning of what's being written, then it's ok …' adds sustenance to a point of view that the expectations of learners' literacy levels is generally low and that the maintenance of literacy standards are of low importance. This in turn is a contributory factor to the problem of poor literacy levels of many people in Britain.

The effect of regional variation on language use is considered in the adult literacy core curriculum (DfES: 116), in the section for Entry 3 level writing, which states under 'Sentence Focus (Grammar and punctuation)' that 'Adults should be taught to: use correct basic grammar', but to 'understand that in some regional varieties of spoken English the subject and verb do not always agree (e.g. *we was, he were*) …'. It goes on to state however that, '… as written English is a non-regional standard, writers use the same written forms wherever they live'. What is not considered however is how subject-verb agreement relates to socio-economic class, and how a learner's spoken English impacts upon their written English and how such issues can be overcome.

Related to the debate surrounding the use of standard or non-standard English grammar, is the debate concerning the importance, or otherwise, of how words are pronounced. Trudgill (1994) gives examples of a range of accent features including 'TH-FRONTING' in words such as 'thing' and 'thought' (pronounced as 'fing' and 'fought') and 'brother' and 'with' (pronounced as 'bruver' and 'wiv') and explains how they come about as a result of 'f' and 'v' being 'pronounced further forward in the mouth. He also gives the example of how the 't' in words such as 'better' and 'bottle' is being pronounced in a 'new way' as a 'GLOTTAL STOP' which he describes as '… a sound which is produced in the larynx, by momentarily closing the vocal cords.' He also explains the way in which such accent features spread across the country and how they are becoming more common amongst the young. Trudgill (1994) argues that such variations and changes in the way words are pronounced are not undesirable. He backs this up through giving examples and explaining how words such as 'thin', when pronounced as 'fin', would not be confused with a fish's fin due to the context in which the word is used. I take his point although there are examples where the context may not be clear and meaning could be confused, for example with the statement, 'I fought very hard'. However, regardless of context, I believe that what is not made clear is the degree to which non-standard grammar and varying pronunciation features relate to social class and impact upon a learner's reading and writing skills.

In terms of the effect of spoken English on reading and writing skills, it should be considered that non-standard speakers may have language related difficulties in developing such skills on the basis that:

> While the English writing system does not directly represent speech…
> the grammar of most varieties of written English is more closely related
> to standard English than to non-standard varieties of spoken English.
>
> **(Wallace 1988: 67)**

However, Wallace (1988: 67) also argues that 'This kind of dialectical mismatch does not appear to be, in itself, a major problem …' whilst others, including Entwhistle (1978) and Bernstein (1964) have argued that those who speak non-standard English fail to benefit to the same degree as standard English speakers from formal education where standard English is the norm.

A number of students who are parents with young children have, over the years, come to my literacy classes and, in the context of discussions on language, said things like, 'my girl comes home from primary school and doesn't say the 't's in Harry 'Potter' [pɒə] and 'water' [wɔːə] and I keep having to correct her!' I then normally ask if the teachers at their child's school correct them themselves to which they normally reply that they're not sure; the fact that students have frequently reported such incidents from a wide range of schools though implies, to me anyway, that it is certainly not standard practice! I've also heard a number of stories from such students saying how their children don't have their punctuation, spelling and grammar checked by their teachers.

I'm often left thinking in such situations, that if parents, and teachers at school, don't correct their children's language at an early age, then the disadvantage caused by the dialectic mismatch between them and their teachers grows. This explains, at least in part, why, as borne out by research, middle class children who start school with lower academic ability than their working class counterparts, soon overtake them, and why it is that the achievement gap between middle class and working class children widens as they progress through the education system.

In my experience, there is a clear correlation between the use of pronunciation features outlined above and the aforementioned non-standard grammar. That doesn't mean to say that all those who make what I regard as 'grammatical errors' speak with any of the pronunciation variations mentioned above. For example, in some dialects, people may simply say 'you was' instead of 'you were' or use 'come' instead of 'came' (for the past simple of the verb 'to come') and make no other grammatical 'errors' nor speak with any of the pronunciation variations stated. However, I find that the greater the degree of regional variation in grammatical forms, the greater is the tendency towards the use of such pronunciation features, or similar, outlined. I'm not suggesting that people from the middle and upper classes don't make 'mistakes' in their spoken grammar or that they don't have their own distinct accent variations, because they do, it's just that the focus here is specifically on those who are at a distinct disadvantage when it comes to learning within the education system and who consequently don't achieve.

The adult literacy core curriculum and the aforementioned national tests in communication, were introduced as part of the government's 'skills for life strategy', launched in 2001, the aim of which is 'to improve the literacy, language and numeracy skills of 1.5m adults in England' by 2007, including young people and adults in low-skilled jobs. However, in spite of much investment, it was reported recently by Smithers (2006) in 'The Guardian' that:

> Up to 16 million adults – nearly half the workforce – are holding down jobs despite having the reading and writing skills expected of children leaving primary school …
>
> **(Smithers 2006: 1)**

This not only begs the question as to what attention is really being made in many of our schools with regard to quite basic literacy and language skills, but also what measures policymakers and OFSTED inspectors are putting in place to ensure all learners develop sufficient literacy and language skills to benefit from, and progress within, their education.

I believe that the attainment of a L1 or L2 test pass is not necessarily evidence in itself of strong numeracy or literacy skills. I say that on the basis that a pass can be achieved with little more than half marks on a multiple choice test. Weak areas in, for example, grammar, punctuation and spelling may still persist, whilst any of the aforementioned issues related to spoken English are not considered

Associated and directly linked with issues regarding grammar and pronunciation, are issues related to the reading skills of learners. There were programmes reflecting concerns over the reading skills of children in schools on the TV during the course of 2008, including for example, 'Lost for Words' and 'Dispatches' ('Why our children can't read' and its follow up, 'Last Chance Kids', both on Channel 4). The programmes emphasised the fact that too many children in our schools either cannot read, or are reading at a level well below that expected for their age. They highlighted such statistics as:

- 1 in 5 leave primary school at the age of 11 not being able to read and write (properly) to the required standard.

- 118,000 finish primary school every year not being able to read, ¾ of them being white working class and 60% of them being boys

- 11% can't read

- 81% leave school at 16

- 35% have no qualifications and so on.

The programmes have illustrated how the return of, and now increased use of, synthetic phonics (which was until recently not the most dominant method for teaching children how to read) to the curriculum has radically improved the reading skills of children, particularly the weakest 25% or so of schools' pupils. It was argued that for those not in the bottom 25%, there was less dependency on the use of any particular method to assist their reading skills and that they could learn from any one method or range of teaching methods deployed.

However, during these TV programmes, there was no apparent correlation made relating to the fact that many of those who struggled with their reading (along with some of the parents of the school children interviewed) had spoken with non-standard dialects and used a high degree of accent variation i.e. made 'errors' in their grammar and pronunciation, such as those discussed earlier. I am not saying that weak grammar and pronunciation is the cause of poor reading (no more than I am saying that it is the cause of illiteracy or street crime or gang culture etc), but it is surely clear that those who speak with non-standard grammar and a high degree of accent variation are disproportionately represented amongst those said people. Synthetics phonics then could provide the opportunity to check on and correct the type of grammatical and pronunciation errors discussed earlier.

Another recent programme featured an award winning secondary school teacher endeavouring to teach a class of adults how to read. In spite of bust ups and students walking out, i.e. obligatory 'made for reality TV' features, the programme showed the teacher successfully deploying synthetic phonics to develop his learners' reading skills, whilst casting aside the adult literacy core curriculum in the process. However, what in my view appeared to be missing, was again any kind of recognition of the fact that all the learners made 'grammatical errors' and used pronunciation variations such as those outlined earlier, in their spoken English. Consequently, the learners' spoken English was not corrected and no correlation was made between their spoken English and their reading and writing skills.

In brief, a synthetic phonics programme starts from what all children learn naturally, the sounds of their own language and teaches them to how to represent those sounds. The programme enables children to practise and learn the underlying skills required to read, namely blending (the ability to 'push' sounds together to build words), segmenting (the ability to pull apart the individual sounds in words) and phoneme manipulation (the ability to insert sounds into, and delete sounds out of, individual words). The programme teaches that these skills are fundamental to being able to use the alphabet code (starting with the initial code and then, when suitably proficient, moving on to the extended code) efficiently in fluent reading and writing. The programme also teaches the conceptual knowledge required to develop those skills i.e. that letters are symbols (graphemes) that represent sounds (phonemes), that the same phonemes can be represented in more than one way and that some graphemes represent more than one sound. With regard to the use of synthetic phonics in teaching adults how to read, I recommend excellent resources entitled 'Phonics Resources for Older Learners' and 'Phonics Stories for Older Learners' (www.forwardwithphonics.com) (Woodward 2012).

The importance of the connection between speaking and listening, and reading and writing is clearly illustrated in a radio 4 interview with Sir Jim Rose, the ex-head of OFSTED, who was commissioned by the Department for Children, Schools and Families to carry out an independent review of the primary curriculum, the largest review of its type for 40 years. During the interview, the focus of which was to explore the affects of 'word poverty' on formal learning, it was recognised that a high percentage of children in some areas of the country started school with such poor language skills and such a limited vocabulary, that they weren't able to start reading, and it was stated that 'reading and writing feed off speaking and listening' and that 'if they can't say it, they can't write it.'

It is apparent that a learner's lack of reading skills clearly disadvantages them in their education, and that this disadvantage deepens as they progress through their education and as the gap between them and those who have more competent reading skills gets wider and wider. I believe that not having access to the use of standard grammar and 'correct' pronunciation (and hence sufficient or relevant language) in the school/educational environment further deepens this disadvantage.

To assist in the development of reading skills, pupils need to be given the opportunity to talk and listen more in the classroom. In so doing, they can be given the chance to express ideas and listen to, and learn from, the ideas of others, whilst providing an opportunity to have their grammar and pronunciation corrected where necessary. This would be of particular benefit to children from lower socio-economic groups who, as stated earlier, often begin their schooling with limited language skills compared with those from more middle class backgrounds.

Year upon year it is reported that soon after formal education begins, bright working-class children fall behind in their education, and although there has been a plethora of research and reports highlighting the fact that pupils from deprived areas under-achieve partly as a result of attending under-performing schools, there has been little in the way, accompanying such research, as to how language and literacy can be used as tools for social equality and advancement for those children from deprived areas.

On that basis; bearing in mind the enormous disadvantages caused by language and reading deficiency, and in order to try and compensate for those disadvantages, I would advocate the introduction of elocution lessons for children at as young an age as possible i.e. during the time they are learning to read (which is usually their first year of compulsory schooling). Naturally, this would need to be done delicately, whilst giving a lot of praise. I know in reality that this may not happen, no matter what arguments are put forward, and that it may be seen as a non starter in principal, even before the issue of logistics, staffing and funding were to be considered. What should happen though is a collective approach amongst policy makers, educationalists and teachers to rigorously correct, as and when necessary, their students' spoken English in terms of their grammar and pronunciation. Many opportunities should be provided for students to talk, within as condusive and relaxed an environment as possible, so that such correction can take place. The teaching of synthetic phonics does, I believe, offer an opportunity for this to occur as it involves making sounds and blending them together. Naturally, the greater the intake of students from lower socio-economic groups, the greater will be the degree of error correction necessary. This will also assist in the National Curriculum's aim, which requires youngsters to be competent in Standard English. The degree of correction will naturally depend on each student's background and the level of spoken English that they bring to the class. It could be just a case of tweaking here and there. It is relatively easy to spot and correct grammatical errors, but those relating to pronunciation are not necessarily so easy to pick up on, but nonetheless important. As mentioned earlier there's a tendency for those from lower socio-economic groups in parts of the country to mispronounce the 'th' as '**f**' in words such as 'think' and 'thought' as '**f**ink' and '**f**ought' or as '**v**' in words such as 'with' and 'bother' as 'wi**v**' and 'bo**v**er'; and to not pronounce the 't' or 'tt' that occurs in the middle of a word (e.g. in la**t**er, compu**t**er, solici**t**or or be**tt**er). The mispronunciation of words, combined with incorrect grammar, are factors which lead to a 'dialectic mismatch' between the student and their teacher and therefore puts the student at a distinct disadvantage, a disadvantage which increases as the student progresses through their education. If there is to be any degree of elocution or correction/tweaking of grammar and pronunciation, then it should be done across all academic subject areas. It needs to be instinctive and carried out with some degree of feeling and passion, and understanding of the rationale behind why it should be done.

It is often argued that language can, and should be, adapted to suit its purpose and audience. For example, in an educational setting we should use more formal language, whilst talking with friends in a social environment more informal language is appropriate. That's fine except most children (and adults) who make consistent grammatical errors and mispronounce some of their words, do not, or are not able to switch from one use of language to another simply because they don't know (or are not aware of) the correct grammar to use and the correct pronunciation of certain words. All this leads to them being disadvantaged. It's important to note then that all the examples we are looking at take place in a formal (educational) setting.

Furthermore, I believe that those who speak non-standard English in terms of their grammar and pronunciation are disproportionately represented amongst those who:

- Are unemployed.

- Have low paid jobs.

- Originate from, and stay within, lower socio-economic groups, and form the underclass of society.

- Are involved in gangs and are perpetrators of crime.

- Are victims of gang-related crime and crime generally.

- Have low literacy levels and struggle to read and write.

- Have limited cultural interests.

- Live in socially deprived areas, and find it more difficult to access services.

Effectively, to make Britain literate, you almost have to overturn a history of class society. I do not claim to be a linguist, I just have a real interest in the subject area and some knowledge through subject specialist teaching (literacy and ESOL) courses and from my own reading and research. It's in part about what I want to hear, and what I believe I should be hearing and how it affects me. It's also about how I believe it affects the culture, life chances and prospects of the individuals I hear and see around me. I wonder to what extent policymakers are exposed and affected by, on a daily basis and over a period of time, to the language of lower working class kids on the streets and in their schools, colleges and workplaces.

Education is not neutral with respect to inequalities in society and any consideration of what is involved in counteracting disadvantage should involve consideration of the origins of different groups of students. It has been argued that education favours middle-class students more than working class students on the basis that their system of values and culture more closely identifies with that of the teachers and the educational system they're in. Add to this arguments by Bernstein (1964), National Commission on Education (1993) and Hoggart (1958), concerning the effects of culture, language aspirations and perceptions on working class children in education, then the size of the disadvantage facing them becomes accentuated. Does not the fact that class society, and its effects upon people's education and life chances, continues to exist in spite of whatever government policies are in force and whatever changes are brought about within the education system as a result, mean that in many ways, one system is the concomitant of another (a case in point being the continued failure of working class children when the 'tripartite system of schooling gave way to comprehensivisation)? Furthermore, it can be argued that it exists because it's functional and the education system at all levels (in spite of whatever changes) functions within it, and no political system really has the ability, will, or even necessarily the need to challenge it. By that I mean that class society as it is lends itself towards a capitalist and/or a socialist system.

In brief, a capitalist system for example relies on a lower working class (or underclass), generally less educated and cultured than the rest, to carry out the more menial jobs, or indeed to be unemployed, and to act as the lower strata of society for the above strata. With only so many professional, skilled and well paid jobs around there is I guess a logic to that. A more Socialist system on the other hand has its roots in the working class, and historically oppressed and marginalised sectors of society. These diverse sectors of society have a culture and the language they use to communicate is part of that culture. To try and amend or criticise that language (even though it would potentially benefit them and increase people's chances of a better education and expose them to a wider culture) is seen as an attack on lower socio-economic groups rather than an attack on the injustices that create them, and generally isn't considered. In other words, within the 'class struggle' itself are the roots of its own demise.

So, in effect, one system is the concomitant of the other in as much there has been no clear cut desire or movement within educational departments of political establishments to challenge or improve the spoken language of the working class. Why else then if you were to trawl the towns and cities of Britain, would you hear so many poorly spoken people, disproportionately represented amongst the inner city schools, FE colleges, single mothers on council estates, workers in traditional working class jobs, the service sector in general, the unemployed, and those involved in gang culture and/or street crime, along with their victims. There are of course many successful working class people, but for every sportsman, businessman, pop star or actor who makes it in their career (and who benefits from the erstwhile commercial exploitation of their culture), many more fail to achieve to anywhere like their full potential, caused, in part, by their lack of language and its effect on their academic and cultural development. But you have, I think, got to hear and feel and experience the lack of language and culture on a regular basis, not like it and want to change it.

I would argue that it is not the so-called middle class system of values that are responsible for the failure of working class children (as is sometimes perceived), more that it is the failure by schools and colleges, and policy makers to bring working class children and their associated culture into line with this middle class system of values (at least in terms of language) that is more likely to blame for their failure in education, since it is the more middle class children who succeed in education. As Zera and Jupp argue:

> If we are serious about including people with a history of educational failure, people for whom Education is a second language, ethnic minority groups, then we have to reproduce for them some of the things that the middle class take for granted. Sooner or later we will have to recognise the lack of a convincing strategy to combat educational failure. Sooner or later the country will have to make changes to the sacrosanct mainstream so that the norms for one group become the opportunities for all.

(Zera and Jupp 2000: 138 & 139)

There seems to be a resistance to this within middle class culture in education based on the notion that one shouldn't be judgemental, undermine or seek to change another class or cultural system of values, whilst at the same time seeing elements of one's own class or culture somehow as a barrier to success of another. This is in part due to a problem that policy makers, managers, educationalists and teachers alike have in education of trying to represent and promulgate a class of people whom they themselves don't identify with. This, combined with the afore-mentioned fact that certain groups have a resistance to education on the basis that they see it as reflecting the values of other social classes, only reinforces the class divide that exists within education and society. Blame, however, doesn't need to be put on middle class values or on working class resistance to education, but neither does a complacent attitude of language use (and its association with class culture) being different but of equal worth, when although very generally speaking, one leads to greater academic success in education and greater levels of attainment in post-16 education and training and greater life chances. Furthermore, I would argue that in looking at the dominant class culture that is represented amongst those who fail in education, ways need to be looked at to change that culture if we consider that in general terms, class society exists as a result of deep rooted historical and social injustices, we must challenge not only the causes of those injustices, but the consequences of the culture produced by those injustices, and not, through policies, educational or otherwise, which don't address the issues, consolidate them or be in denial of them.

So, from the teacher educators (who speak and use standard English, yet promulgate the use of non-standard English through not correcting it sufficiently), to the indifferent speakers of standard English to the low skilled worker and unemployed people (who use non-standard English), many of those in potential positions of influence are collectively responsible for the low level of expectations in terms of literacy standards of many people in this country and the concomitant low literacy levels of those people.

Pupils should not only be able to work comfortably at a reasonable level of literacy long before they leave secondary school, the importance of being literate to this degree should be installed into them long before they leave secondary school. The fact that in my job role, I observe on a daily basis that many of the learners I work with are not able to speak (or write) in standard English, I believe is a fairly clear sign that like it or not, the argument has been lost.

One of the reasons so many people have difficulties in spelling, punctuation and grammar is because they have not had basic rules consistently reinforced throughout their schooling. This lack of consistency then continues through, as stated earlier, into further education. Look around any college of further education and listen to how many of the full time learners speak among themselves. If they've recently been through 11 years of education without having their grammar or pronunciation consistently corrected (and all that that entails relating to their literacy and communication skills), then it's very unlikely they'll respond to much of a degree now, or be encouraged to reflect upon and adapt their spoken English (again with all that that entails relating to their literacy and communication skills). Somehow it just isn't seen as important, and people can even be at best indifferent, and at worst scornful, of attempts to even raise the issue. As mentioned earlier, it's not a case of wanting learners to 'talk posh' amongst themselves, it's about learners, within an educational or professional environment, being able to utilise Standard English, whether through speaking or writing (or both) for their own advantage, and hence not being disadvantaged.

I believe that language use is determined by one's socio-economic status or social group (as well as age and gender), and the context in which the language is used. However, I also believe that in order for literacy to be a tool for providing greater equality of opportunity for some social groups, then the effects of non-standard English use on the educational achievements of those social groups needs to be given greater consideration. Promoting the principal of Equality of Opportunity isn't enough when what is required for the provision of equality of opportunity is not understood or provided for. The results of this lack of understanding are all too apparent when we see the consequences for the many people who are left behind.

Although there has been a plethora of research and reports highlighting the fact that pupils from deprived areas under-achieve partly as a result of attending under-performing schools, there has been little in the way, accompanying such research, as to how language and literacy can be used as tools for social equality and advancement for those children from deprived areas.

Returning then to the argument as to whether or not the use of standard English should be enforced in schools, it is clear from listening to many of the children within our inner-city schools and students within FE colleges, that the argument in favour of standard English has been lost.

What I perceive of as poor or incorrect grammar and pronunciation is passed on from generation to generation within the home environment. Pupils entering the education system using non-standard English leave it several years later (whether it be school, FE college or training provider) having rarely (if at all) had their use of non-standard spoken English challenged or corrected in circumstances where it should have been, a factor which contributes significantly to the cycle of failure that many users of non-standard English enter.

A serious debate needs to be started over the issue of spoken English and literacy within schools and post-16 education providers. If literacy standards do not increase substantially, then any ideas expressed have failed, whether or not they were ever considered in the first place, as indeed were any previous initiatives.

In conclusion, I am advocating the following:

- Elocution and/or constant correction of grammar and pronunciation, beginning in primary school and continuing through secondary and post-16 education.

- Greater use of talking and listening activities in primary schools in order to develop vocabulary, speaking skills and confidence in expressing ideas.

- Constant correction of spelling, punctuation and grammar (appropriate to pupils' levels) within English classes during primary school, across the curriculum throughout secondary education and within all academic and vocational areas in post-16 education. The latter point will in turn help to develop parity of esteem between the academic and vocational areas, post-16.

- The development and introduction of learning assessments to replace SATS within primary and secondary schools, and to replace current literacy initial and diagnostic assessments within post-16 institutions.

- Connected with the above points, all those involved directly in education to have higher expectations of learners' literacy levels.

The main focus of this is book isn't so much about resources for developing literacy skills, as there is an abundance of good resources available from many quarters, it's more about setting a framework for the potential development of language and literacy skills. Such a framework includes, in the context of educational settings, greater awareness of the importance spoken language (grammar and pronunciation) and its association with the development of learners' literacy skills, and all that entails in terms of providing a greater access to curricula and a wider culture, and hence better life chances. It does however contain a literacy learning assessment (referred to earlier), along with a rationale for its use, and a range of related resources.

In this second edition, further resources have been added with a particular focus on the reading and writing components of functional skills. The resources include a range of Functional Skills reading comprehension and writing exercises, supported by discussion-based articles and letter writing exercises, along with an analysis of word classes. The discussion-based articles adopt an 'integrated' approach whereby a wider vocabulary, along with a knowledge and understanding of word classes, punctuation features, and spelling, and how they are related, is promoted.

In the academic year 2010/2011, functional skills were rolled out across education providers as an essential element in the four qualification routes for young people from 14 to 19; in apprenticeships, GCSE, in the new Diploma, and the Foundation Learning Tier, as well as being stand-alone qualifications in their own right. They are regarded by Government as the core elements of English, mathematics and ICT that provide young people and adults with the skills and abilities they need to participate effectively and independently in life, learning and work, and have been introduced in order to address employers' concerns that young people and adults have not been achieving a firm enough grounding in the basics.

The People's Book Prize
After this book was first published in 2009, the book was entered for a new book competition called 'The People's Book Prize' (TPBP), whereby the public voted for their favourite book each month (for fiction, non-fiction and children's) with each month's winners going through to the final, with the public again voting on line, the winners of which were announced in an awards ceremony at the Stationers Hall on July 21st 2010, near St Paul's Cathedral, London. The

book got through to the final, through having the most votes in the non-fiction category for the month of February, 2010, although it didn't win on the night. On the night itself, following a lavish, 3-course meal (at the discounted price of £85 for the finalists!) the presentations for the awards began. The non-fiction prize was conducted first; as each of the 12 finalists was announced, they had to stand up, me being one of them. The presenter talked for a while longer to build up the suspense; it was my 'Strictly' or 'X-factor' moment! I didn't win. When the ceremony was completed, I walked over to the winner, smiled gracefully, summoned as much sincerity as I could muster, shook his hand and congratulated him.

As mentioned, the prize was given to the book with the most on-line votes. I was very conscious of the fact that in the few weeks voting time leading up to the Awards Ceremony, I had been quite a pain, asking friends, family, students and colleagues as well as a range of people I barely knew. Of course, as the number of votes each author obtains in the competition relates to the number of people he or she asks, begs or sends emails to, it raises the question of the validity of such a prize. Most other better known book prizes are awarded, of course, as a result of decisions made by a panel of expert judges. However, it could be questioned as to whether or not the degree to which the writers they judge are able to stimulate, encourage and develop people's interest in, and access to, reading and literacy standards should be considered.

Sadly, the Founding Patron of TPBP, the writer Dame Beryl Bainbridge, who was to award the prizes on the evening, died of cancer just 2 weeks before the awards ceremony. It was mentioned during the award ceremony during tributes to her how much she had endorsed and supported the vision of a book prize to promote unknown writers who had had their work published through independent publishers.

I felt a personal irony too. After news of her untimely death was announced on Radio 4's PM programme on Friday, July 9th, a clip was played of her from an interview a couple of years earlier, lamenting the decline of spoken English in this country, and placing the blame, in part, on the education system and the popularity of soap operas. Whilst her opinions were a reflection of how she felt about spoken English within her native Liverpool, she clearly advocated, during the interview, the introduction of elocution lessons into all state schools!

Principal's speech

On one occasion, I heard the principal of a college where I previously worked, address his staff at a meeting. During the meeting, he said that as a college, we should be tough on students' language generally in order to improve their employability and opportunities, and that if bad language was tolerated in college, students would be at a disadvantage in the 'real world' of the job market. I certainly agreed with this sentiment in principle, although knew from experience that examples of staff challenging the use of students' bad language were rare, and for understandable reasons, when considering the personal abuse such efforts can frequently invoke. In reality, such ideas, however well intentioned, rarely, if ever, get implemented. I wanted him (and heads of all educational establishments) to go much further than advocating the challenging of bad language though; what I've been advocating for some time is that all teachers should, when necessary, routinely correct their students' language, but I don't mean just their 'bad language', but their pronunciation and grammar. This would ensure, I believe, that all students would be able to have better access to the curriculum being taught, and hence better access to more advanced studies and to the job market.

Secondment

In 2011, due to the retirement of a colleague, I obtained a 0.5 secondment to the Teacher Training department. In the course handbook, I noticed one of the books on the recommended reading list was 'Eats, Shoots and Leaves' by Lynn Truss, a well-known and successful book in the field of education in general and literacy in particular. The book is well known, as it states on its cover, for taking a 'zero tolerance' approach to punctuation. The book explains in quite clear detail how incorrect punctuation can alter the meaning of text or make a piece of writing incoherent and, by definition, grammatically incorrect. During that time, most of which I found challenging, but rewarding, I taught a couple of the final year modules on the Cert Ed (Certificate in Education) programme. Whilst marking some of the students' assignments for the modules, I found that in some cases, punctuation was 'all over the place' making the text incoherent. As a result, I felt that the criteria had not been met and therefore referred some assignments, giving constructive feedback and explanations in the process. Whilst some learners were able to recognise and acknowledge where they had made punctuation and grammatical errors (and in many cases spelling and typing errors too) and how it affected meaning, and hence whether or not they had met certain criteria, and were happy to go ahead and make the relevant corrections, with guidance if necessary, others were less inclined to accept such decisions and preferred instead to complain, in some cases quite vociferously, on the basis that I had not assessed the criteria. Unfortunately for me however, I was called to account for decisions I had made. I guess the point I'm making is the degree to which the zero tolerance advocated by Truss is in reality a limited tolerance of correcting punctuation! If teacher trainers aren't encouraged to emphasise the importance of literacy standards and freely correct trainee teachers I thought, then the degree to which those teachers, once qualified, will emphasise the importance of literacy standards and freely correct their students will be considerably limited. In my opinion, there is a clear correlation between the low level of expectations on teachers' literacy levels, and the consequent low level of expectations on students' literacy levels along with the wide differential that exists in literacy levels between students, of all ages.

It is generally understood, and expected, in teaching that those who are delivering a particular subject should themselves be well qualified in that subject, and at the very least, be one level above the students they are teaching. However, during my experience in the post-16 sector, I have observed that many of the tutors delivering functional skills English do not have a level 3 literacy qualification. Furthermore, in terms of the entry requirements onto Cert Ed courses, it is my understanding that there is no minimum literacy) level entry requirement for trainee teachers, although there is meant to be a requirement to achieve a level 2 literacy qualification by the end of the training. However, this can be achieved by passing a 40 question multiple choice level 2 adult literacy test with just over half marks!

To deal with the competition in the job market within the context of today's economic climate, I've heard reports of employers demanding that in order to get on an apprenticeship programme, applicants need to have 4 good GCSEs (i.e. grades A – C), including maths and English, in order to be considered. It seems rather odd to me then, that in order to get onto a teaching programme, the bare minimum level of English and maths is not required (i.e. a level 2 GCSE 'equivalent' qualification), yet in order to be considered for an apprenticeship programme, GCSEs in both maths and English are becoming necessary!

I have argued on many occasions, over a period of years, that any tutor delivering literacy should themselves have a level 3 (or above) literacy qualification and that a level 2 literacy qualification should be part of a stringent admissions policy for teachers entering the post-16 sector, and that that qualification should either be a GCSE in English (grade A – C) or a level 2 functional English qualification (but not a less rigorous level 2 adult literacy qualification.

The issues raised above don't just happen though; standards, and the expectations of learners', and teachers', numeracy levels don't just decline, and as such, the context in which they have, needs to be reflected on. People have opposed the decline in standards, and called for higher expectations of learners and teachers. In meetings within a variety of educational establishments and at various levels, decisions to allow tutors to deliver Functional Skills English to a level they barely have themselves, and to allow teachers onto, and to complete, teacher education courses with a low level of literacy skills have all been opposed. My understanding is that many students across the country are struggling to pass the level 2 functional skills English exam, particularly the writing component. I believe that the correlation between poor results, and the low level of expectations of teachers' and learners' literacy skills is evident.

It's not just teacher trainers and their managers that are responsible for failing to ensure basic literacy levels amongst teachers, and therefore students, one also has to question the role of OFSTED, who are responsible for the regulation of the education system, in allowing low literacy standards to go unchallenged both within the compulsory, and post-compulsory education, sector, and the role of the Institute for Learning, the professional body for the Further Education and Skills sector, in failing to demand a higher level literacy and numeracy qualification for entry into its organisation and from its members in order to achieve QTLS status (Qualified Teacher Learning and Skills), and to advocate a higher level literacy and numeracy standard for entry onto teacher training courses.

Furthermore, in light of evidence from undercover reporters in late 2011 showing examiners from examining boards coaching teachers how to increase pupils' marks, and extolling the virtues of pupils having to learn less with their particular examining board, the role of examining boards and the way they are regulated needs to be questioned, as does the way in which they have linked up with textbook producers.

My own apostrophe story

A few years ago, I needed to renew my passport quite quickly, so booked an appointment at the passport office near Victoria Station for its Fast Track service. I arrived at the office a bit early, and was told by a security guard to wait outside until my appointment time. Whilst outside, I read a security notice on the door which stated, 'Please leave your bag and it's contents in the appropriate area.' When inside the building at around my appointment time, I pointed the error out to a woman at the reception desk, who then looked at me as if I was crazy! I often tell this story, as part of my repertoire, to my literacy classes. I also frequently talk about the importance of the correct use of correct punctuation, grammar and spelling etc. However, I frequently feel like I'm facing a losing battle when I see so many errors around me in everyday life which go unchallenged and become acceptable, and even more so within the context of, as mentioned earlier, the issue of the failure of teachers, and teaching assistants, to constantly and consistently correct students' punctuation, spelling and grammar throughout their schooling.

Newspapers

In my opinion, in terms of quality of writing, The Observer is one of the best Sunday newspapers whereas the News of The World (before it ceased circulation), in spite of some of its clever, investigative journalism and the fact that, like other newspapers its writers were able to write shrewdly at the appropriate level for its readers, was one of the worst. However, in terms of their respective circulations, the News of the World sold on average around 3 million copies every Sunday as compared with 0.28 million copies for The Observer. This then raises the question of why it is that so many people don't have the literacy skills, and connected to this the interest, to engage in the reading of a newspaper like the Observer, and why it is that such a newspaper isn't, through its journalism i.e. its research and reporting, encouraging and promoting such engagement through pressurising and influencing government policy makers to introduce measures to ensure a fair greater proportion of the population have the literacy skills, and interest, to engage in the reading of such newspapers, and to scrutinise and learn from, its articles.

One can frequently read reports and articles in newspapers (for example, some of those included in the discussion-based articles) decrying literacy standards in this country, often in a matter of fact way due to their frequency; one can, of course, without looking too hard, also come across directly, in everyday life, examples of low levels of literacy whether in an educational, work or any other setting. However, the 'cutting edge' for me is in the context of the meetings whereby people raising the issue of standards, and coming forward with genuine, radical ideas of how to raise them, are marginalised and ignored in favour of the status quo, or minor, insignificant policy adjustments.

If we consider literacy in its wider context i.e. in the context of the interface between education and the wider world, then there's no end to the number of issues in society that can be taken on board:

Summer Riots, 2011

I missed the summer riots in August 2011, due to a flight to Johannesburg on Sunday, August 7th for a holiday back in Southern Africa. The protests had already begun in Tottenham though, which I'd followed with a keen interest, in part because I'd lived and worked there for a few years, teaching applied science at the College of North East London. When I arrived in Johannesburg, I was met by an old Zambian friend living there. We went out that first night and, in spite of its reputation as one of the most dangerous cities in the world, saw no trouble at all, and felt quite safe. This is in stark contrast by the way to the time I lived and taught in Botswana when my trips through Southern Africa seemed forever fraught with danger (but that's for another time and book). Anyway, when we got back to my friend's house in Kelvin (ironic in a way, since when I lived in Africa, many African people used to mispronounce my name as Kelvin), we turned on a South African News channel and watched the riots in Britain on the telly! 'Something's wrong here', I said to my friend, 'I'm just so used to it being the other way round, sitting in a house in England and watching, or reading about, riots in Africa!'

Anyway, not long after arriving back in the UK, I received a generic email from the BBC inviting me to apply for tickets for a debate on the riots, organised by Radio 4's Today programme, at the Birmingham Town Hall, on Monday evening, September 5th. So, I applied on-line for a ticket, was luckily awarded one, and travelled up to Birmingham by train for the debate, along with 900 or so other people. The debate, which was chaired by James Naughtie, was led on the platform by 3 panels of 5 people (mainly local dignitaries and youth social workers etc), an hour or so being allocated to each panel, including time for audience questions and comments. Many issues were raised and discussed during the debate relating to the causes of the riots and the best way forward following them, some quite vociferously, as one would imagine. Among them, the issue of the correlation between unemployment and the lack of employability skills, including literacy and numeracy, amongst the young, was raised by members of one of the panels. At this point, I jotted down a question of my own, which was along the lines of:

"One thing, I believe,the majority of rioters had in common was poor communication, language and literacy skills. As Jim Rose, the ex-head of OFSTED stated when you [James Naughtie] interviewed him in 2010, 'reading and writing feed directly off speaking and listening.' Young people who offend often have poorly developed verbal skills which can make reasoning with others difficult. On that basis, do you think it would be a good idea, as part of the way forward, to introduce elocution, or at least constant and consistent error correction of children's grammar and pronunciation etc. from an early age, as advocated by the late Beryl Bainbridge, in order that they can have greater access to learning, qualifications, achievement, employment and, ultimately, greater self-esteem, and if so, do you think that this, in turn, would lead to both a reduction in the need of those young people to riot and in the disparities between the haves and have-nots? I obviously do, and have been arguing for it over a period of years". Unfortunately, perhaps being aware of the fact that the highlights of the debate were to be broadcast on the Today programme the following morning, combined with the fear of becoming tongue-tied in front of a large audience, I bottled out of asking the question!

Street crime

Reflecting on the high profile street crime that appears on our news screens (in particular, youth knife and gun crime etc), when people, who are normally associated with the victim, are interviewed (be it family, friends or people in the neighbourhood etc), a disproportionate number of them come across as not well educated, which is reflected in the way they speak through the use of incorrect grammar and pronunciation, and lack of suitable vocabulary to express themselves. It is clear then that a disproportionate number of victims of street crime are represented in those from lower socio-economic backgrounds. This would also, in most cases, be the situation with regards the perpetrators; although naturally one doesn't get to hear them being interviewed so often, one sometimes needs to make reasonable judgements or 'educated guesses' based on their own experiences and encounters.

Looking at a specific example, In March 2010, it was reported on the news that a 17 year old teenager was stabbed to death at Victoria Tube Station by a large gang of youths, during the day and in front of horrified commuters, and that 12 teenagers (a mix of 16 and 17 year olds), some still at school, had subsequently been arrested. It occurred to me that if I was to meet them in an English or literacy class, and ask them to write something like, 'We weren't there at the tube station yesterday knifing a teenage boy to death', then not only would most of them not be able to write out the sentence correctly, but many of them would not be able to say it correctly; in spite of eleven years or so of compulsory education. Arguments persist however, that it's not necessary for teachers to consistently correct children's written and spoken English, and acknowledge the correlation between the two. 'How do you define speaking correctly anyway?' or similar, is a question sometimes put forward, and with a particular challenging tone, which negates further discussion or understanding. Failure of the working class, it seems, is deeply rooted in the education system.

Nursery staff and childminders

In late March 2012, the interim findings of a review into early years' education and childcare qualifications (the Nutbrown Review) reported that nursery staff and child minders were being allowed to work at pre-school groups without demonstrating even basic literacy or literacy skills. This of course begs the question of why this has been discovered only now, and why it needed a 'review' to find these things out when everyday observations, common sense and basic initiative could have easily lead to the same conclusions long ago.

In a way, I thought, at least there's a consistency that completes the circle i.e. the low expectations of preschool employees matching the low level of expectations of trainee teachers in the post-16 sector! However, it is often those who are least able to challenge such low levels of expectations (i.e. the parents and guardians of the preschool children, and the young learners in the post-16 sector) who are generally most affected. In my opinion though, it's a real disgrace that such a low level of expectations of preschool employees' literacy and numeracy skills has been allowed to become the 'norm.'

The deputy principal's speech

It was during a whole college staff meeting in January '12 that the deputy principal of the FE college where I was working at the time stated that in future inspections, OFSTED would be seeking evidence that tutors were checking for spelling, punctuation and grammar.

Would they, I thought, be checking for tutors' spelling, punctuation and grammar and more importantly, I thought, why was there ever a situation when OFSTED weren't concerned about whether or not tutors were checking their learners' spelling, punctuation and grammar! Clutching for analogies, I remembered an old Monty Python sketch where a football game is played between teams of Greek and German philosophers. For the first eighty nine minutes of the game, the philosophers walk around in circles contemplating theories of reality etc when, with just one minute remaining, Archimedes has a 'Eureka' moment and kicks the ball towards the goal, crosses it to Socrates who scores with a diving header. The referee awards a goal, in spite of Hegel arguing that the reality is merely an a priori adjunct of non-naturalistic ethics, and Karl Marx protesting that it was offside! OFSTED then I thought, if they are only now starting to check for evidence that tutors are checking for spelling, punctuation and grammar, could be added to the list of those responsible for low literacy standards in this country.

I've given here, in the previous few pages, only a small sample of examples of how there is an entrenched acceptance of low literacy standards and the failure of the working class across many sectors of society, including Government and opposition parties, educationalists and policy makers, but clearly they're all connected. I believe that such acceptance is so ingrained into our society that it's become nearly impossible to address the issue constructively, even when attempts are made to draw attention to the subject at various levels. It's hard to believe that such low expectations and standards could be tolerated, but when seen in another context i.e. the potential threat a literate and numerate society could be to the power and privilege of various sections of the establishment, and of those that oppose it, then it begins to make a bit more sense.

Across the country, the correlation between people's professions, along with their social class and income, and the way they speak is apparent. This divide is reflected in people's cultural interests too. This serves a purpose in maintaining social order and hierarchies. The further people are apart culturally, the less likely they are to mix and understand one another's outlooks, and when people don't mix and understand one another, they don't unite; ideal for maintaining the status quo. I'm generalising greatly here of course, but I believe, when you add up all the evidence, only a small part of which I have attempted to address in this book, that there is something in this line of argument.

One of the main points I'm making in the above texts, and in the letters on pages 115–119, is that If we lived in a society where high literacy and numeracy skills are normal, or taken for granted, then people would be much more readily able, and likely, to engage in issues that directly, or indirectly, relate to the their own lives, and the lives of others, whether concerning employment, the state of the economy, pensions, the banking crisis, distribution of taxes, social breakdown and disorder, the effects of technological developments on our lives, arms sales, education or the NHS etc. and in so doing begin to challenge the many injustices that occur in our society.

Being proved wrong, and made a fool of, is not something I would relish and nor, of course, would most people. However, if the opportunity were to arise, and in order for me to get this argument out of my system, I would relish a genuine challenge, such as outlined in the following scenario:

A thousand or so adults from a working class background of varying ages, and from different parts of the country etc. are chosen at random, and asked if they think it would be a good idea to introduce elocution lessons into state schools, or if they think it would have been a good idea for them to have had elocution lessons when they were at school. If the majority of people were to answer 'no' then I would probably just count my losses and skulk away, but if they were to say 'yes', then I believe there would be an argument to pursue!

Rationale behind the Literacy Learning Assessments and literacy resources

Like the numeracy learning assessment, the literacy learning assessments focus on areas of difficulty that many learners face, and give the learner (facilitated by a tutor) the opportunity to dovetail into areas of required learning through the assessment and feedback process. Also (again like the numeracy learning assessment) it replaces the need for initial and diagnostic assessments (where no learning takes place) with an integrated practical learning assessment (where learning can take place) which is routed in the context of having high expectations of all learners. The learning assessments are offered at 2 levels, a judgement being needed by a tutor as to which one would be more appropriate for any given learner. They allow tutors to develop skills in providing effective and focused feedback to learners and in so doing, provide learning opportunities for them. Leading on from the feedback, the learning assessments can be used and developed as learning resources. With current paper-based and computer-based initial and diagnostic assessments, there is no real involvement in the learning process by the tutor, the assessment being manually (or automatically) marked, followed by a level being administered, which is a process requiring little skill. Although a marking scheme and time limit for the assessment are suggested, it can be regarded as flexible, as indeed can the makeup and/or weighting of the questions and assignment of a level to a given mark. On the one hand a need for the assignation of a level can be required for purposes of differentiation between learners, on the other, the focus of the learning assessments, it should be remembered, should be on providing the opportunity to learn. Rather than an area of difficulty being diagnosed as 'spelling', a tutor may be able to determine more specifically from the 'dictated sentences' and 'free writing' parts of the literacy learning assessments the types or patterns of spelling error made by the learner and offer solutions through reinforcing of spelling rules, identifying spelling patterns and providing the opportunity for repetition of those patterns. These areas of difficulty may include:

- Understanding of spelling rules in words such as 'families' ('y' → 'ies' when forming plurals) and 'receive' ('e' before 'i' after a 'c').

- Misuse of homophones (same sounding words such as there/their; here/ hear; too/to; your/you're etc).

- Omission of letters such as the first 'e' in different (and difference), the 'c' in 'excellent' or the 'r' in surprise, as they are often not pronounced.

- Failing to omit the 'e' when adding the 'ing' suffix to a verb e.g. 'write' to 'writing' or 'take' to 'taking' etc.

- Doubling of the consonant when adding a suffix to a short (or 1 syllable) verb e.g. 'run' to 'running'; 'let' to letting 'plan' to 'planned' etc.

The grammar exercises enable the learner to focus on some of the most common everyday spoken grammatical errors which can be reflected in written English. These errors include the use of double negatives, and 'was' for 'were', 'done' for 'did' and 'come' for 'came' in past tenses. In addition, the literacy learning assessment assesses a wide range of literacy skills (including 'reading for understanding' and 'free writing') whilst allowing the learner to utilise a range of learning styles. In marking and providing feedback to the learner, experience can be gained in identifying and correcting types of spelling, punctuation and grammatical errors made by learners (and in so doing, address an action point frequently raised in external verification key skills reports and issues addressed in the aforementioned, 'Working on the 3 Rs').

The literacy learning assessments focus on developing everyday literacy skills and (as with the numeracy learning assessment), is contextualised and gives learners the opportunity to learn from the assessment itself, including from their own mistakes.

The literacy learning assessments consist of the following 4 areas:

- Spelling (including homophones)

- Grammar

- Reading for understanding (including vocabulary in context,

- punctuation, comprehension and main purpose of text)

- Free writing

With regards to the free writing exercise, one of the areas of difficulty that learners face is the ability to write in complete sentences. A typical error that learners make, for example, is to use commas instead of full stops at the end of sentences. Exercises such as 'Full Stops and Capital Letters', which focus on where sentences end, can be used to overcome this issue, along with everyday reading of a range of suitable texts, whilst adapting to the punctuation appropriately, and further free writing practice.

Another issue facing learners is the ability to develop complex sentences from simple or compound ones through the use of conjunctions such as when, because, if, whenever, whilst etc. Such conjunctions, when used, turn sentences into complex ones through the formation of a subordinate clause (which does not make sense on its own) accompanying a main clause (which does make sense on its own). For example:

The minibus arrived late because it was delayed by the traffic.

Here, '*The minibus arrived late*' is the main clause, as it can stand on its own and make sense, whilst '*because it was delayed by traffic*' is the subordinate clause, as it does not make sense on its own. To assist in addressing this issue, exercises to locate and highlight simple, compound and complex sentences within a range of text, including those within the dictated sentences, can be carried out as well as exercises choosing the appropriate conjunction to join two simple sentences, and indicating the main and subordinate clauses. In addition, learners should be encouraged, and given the opportunity, to use complex sentences (along with simple and compound ones) within the context of free writing exercises.

Although the focus of any particular exercise may be on one main aspect of literacy, such as spelling, grammar, reading for overall understanding, scanning for particular information, developing vocabulary or punctuation etc, where possible, other aspects of literacy can be highlighted. Naturally, both within, and outside of, the educational setting, learners should be encouraged to read and engage with written material, be it books, newspapers or magazines) as much as possible. Within the context of the above, the reading of specific, relevant and engaging articles can lend itself to exercises which highlight the use of correct spelling, punctuation and grammar within the text. Such articles can also be used to develop learners' knowledge of unfamiliar vocabulary and phrases or expressions (relating to, for example, specific technical or scientific language which the learners may not be familiar with) in preparation for discussion based around the whole article.

In conclusion, I believe that the facilitation of learning assessments would be an effective way to both develop learners' literacy skills and to support tutors and/or vocational coaches in supporting their learners. Leading on from the learning assessment, a tutor should be able to deliver learning relating to spelling, punctuation, grammar, vocabulary, sentence structure and understanding of text etc using a range of resources.

Although it's a situation I come across frequently, it rarely ceases to surprise me when I'm asked questions such as, 'What's a verb?' or 'What's a noun?' or 'What's an adjective?' It surprises me because it appears that schooling has in many cases not embedded such knowledge into its pupils sufficiently in spite of the fact that an understanding of such terms can aid grammar, punctuation and spelling and in spite of the fact that such questions can be explained to, and/or elicited from a learner within a relatively short period of time through the use of definitions and short explanations such as:

A **word class** (or **part of speech**) is a grammatical group into which words can be divided. The main ones, which students should be aware of, can be summarised as follows:

A **noun** is a word that refers to an object (or thing), event, substance or state. A noun can stand alone with an article (i.e. with 'a', 'an' or 'the' before it). For example:

The **books** were under the **table**. The **choice** wasn't easy. I've got a great **idea**.

He said that he had a strange **dream** last **night**. The **beauty** of it all was amazing.

It was a great **occasion** and everyone had an enjoyable **time**.

She occasionally went jogging before **breakfast**.

A **proper noun** refers to a place or person. For example: Manchester, Craig, Highbury, Julia.

A **pronoun** is a word which is used instead of a noun, and is sometimes used to refer to a noun or common noun that has already been mentioned. For example:

John took part in the karaoke, but I don't think **he** enjoyed it that much. **They** appreciated all the support they received. The play was quite good, although I think **it** went on a bit too long. We were the ones **who** started the project.

A **verb** is a word or phrase that describes an action, condition or experience. It changes according to person (i.e. who, or what, carries out the action etc.) and tense (i.e. when the action is carried out etc. For example:

He **felt** better afterwards. She **runs** every day. It**'s raining** cats and dogs They **have been** there on several occasions. He **described** the play to him.

The tanks **role** by every minute. The dogs **seemed** hungry.

They **will go** there in the morning.

An **adjective** is a word that describes a noun or pronoun. For example:

The **kind**, **young** man sat on the **wooden** stool. He looked past the **old** house towards the row of **short**, **green** trees. He was **tall** and **slim**. The dogs seemed **hungry**. He had a **strange** dream. I've got a **great** idea. John was told to be **careful** after losing his laptop for the **second** time. Due to his illness, Fred wasn't a **well** man.

An **adverb** is a word that describes or gives more information about a verb or adjective. For example:

The old man drove **slowly** down the long, bumpy road. They slept **well** last night.

She thought **carefully** about her future. They felt passionately about the game.

She has driven **cautiously** since receiving the speeding fine.
He **seriously** considered quitting his job. He felt **better** after taking the medicine.
The town was **surprisingly** large. Mr Murdoch was **immensely** rich.

A **conjunction** is a word that connects words, phrases and clauses in a sentence:

Elton waited in the café **while** his wife did the shopping.
They enjoyed their holiday **although** the weather was awful.
He got into his car **and** drove away quickly.
She liked the scenery and the people and the people **but** wasn't so keen on the food.

A **preposition** is a word which is used before a noun, or a pronoun, connecting it to another word. It often donates direction or position. For example:

He walked **through** the alleyway, **down** the street, **past** the post office, **over** the bridge and **through** the alleyway until finally he arrived **at** the car park. When he was there, he got **into** his car and placed the box he had been carrying **on** the passenger seat.

Prepositions also donate time and possession. For example:

He left **after** he had made his speech, but **before** anyone in the audience had a chance to ask any questions. With his head still full **of** ideas, he went to the bar and ordered a cup **of** coffee.

Of course, practice needs to be given and explanations reinforced over a period of time. Sentences, such as the following, along with associated exercises can be used frequently to illustrate the aforementioned word classes:

"The young man drove quickly down the long, bumpy road."

Nouns:	man, road
Verbs:	drove (past of the verb 'to drive')
Adjectives:	young (describes the man), long and bumpy (describes the road)
Adverbs:	quickly (describes how the man drove)
Conjunctions:	
Prepositions:	down
Pronoun:	

"She went to a good college, but didn't finish her course"

Nouns:	college, course
Verbs:	went, finish, didn't (auxiliary verb)
Adjectives:	good
Adverbs:	
Conjunctions:	but
Prepositions:	to
Pronoun:	She, her

When introducing and discussing the topic of word classes with students in my literacy classes, I go out of my way to explain that on the one hand, they won't, rather incredibly, ever be tested on their knowledge of them in any English test, yet on the other hand, if they do have a good working knowledge and understanding of them, then it will assist greatly in their overall understanding of their own language, as well as their spelling, punctuation and grammar. I also state that in my experience, those learners who do have an overall understanding of word classes, in general have a better ability to spell, punctuate and use correct grammar, as well as having a wider knowledge of vocabulary and understanding of text. I emphasise that the fact that in my opinion, it is a travesty that there is little or no expectation on people to understand word classes i.e. to know about the structure of their own language.

The knowledge of word classes can, for example, be linked to punctuation. Where 2 nouns appear together (or a common noun followed by a noun), the first noun will end in an 's' and have an apostrophe before or after it, depending on whether it is singular or plural, to indicate possession of the second noun. When this is the case, the nouns can be rearranged in order to show, and further explain, the possession. For example:

The **student's jacket** was on the table = The **jacket of the student** was on the table.

John's idea didn't go down well with his audience = **The idea of John** didn't go down well with his audience.

The **children's bicycles** were in the shed = The **bicycles of the children** were in the shed.

The **boy's games** were in his room = The **games of the boy** were in his room.

The **boys' consoles** were in their play area = The **consoles of the boys** were in their play area.

The **lady's scarf** was left on the coat hanger = The **scarf of the lady** was left on the coat hanger.

The **ladies' jackets** were left in the cloakroom = The **jackets of the ladies** were left in the cloakroom.

The article will appear in next **week's newspaper** = The article will appear in **the newspaper of next week.**
The stream was just a **stone's throw** away from the back of his garden = The stream was just **the throw of a stone** away from the back of his garden.

In the context of word classes, it can be further explained that if the word is a verb and it ends in an 's' or 'es' then it cannot have an apostrophe as verbs themselves don't possess anything. Several (but not all) adverbs end in 'ly' and can be formed by adding the 'ly' to the adjective, for example:

She gave a **beautiful** performance. Here, 'beautiful' is an adjective as it's describing a performance (a noun).
She sang beautiful**ly**. Here, 'beautifully' is an adverb as it's describing how she sang (a verb).
Phil and Diana were mugged as they walked home from the train station after dark. After that, they were both very **cautious**. Here, 'cautious' is an adjective as it's describing the pronoun 'they' i.e. Phil and Diana.
They drove cautious**ly** through the mist and rain. Here, 'cautiously' is an adverb as it's describing how they drove (a verb).

Word classes should be reinforced periodically, for example through selecting words following the reading of discussion based articles, and testing learners' knowledge. In addition, several useful resources relating to word classes can be found on literacy websites such as bbcskillswise. For example, there are exercises to place words from texts into the correct word class category, and exercises to create nouns from verbs (and vice-versa), which can also be used to test for, and develop, learners' vocabulary knowledge and spelling.

L1 Learning Assessment (Literacy)

Name: _____   **Date:** _____

The purpose of the assessment is to check any weak areas you may have, but more importantly to give you the chance to learn from it, and to develop everyday literacy skills. At the end of the assessment you can take away a copy of your paper together with an answer sheet to learn from.
Time allowed for the assessment: 30 minutes

Mark: _____   Level: _____
    40

Spelling (12)

Six sentences will be dictated to you by your tutor or vocational coach:

1. _____

2. _____

3. _____

4. _____

5. _____

6. _____

Grammar Exercise (8)

The following conversation between 2 people (A and B) contains some of the most common grammatical errors made in everyday spoken English. There are 8 errors in total, and they are underlined. Place the correct word above.
e.g. 'I done' is incorrect. It should be 'I did'.

A   'Have you done any courses here before?'

B   'Yes, I did a sports therapy course here last year.'

A 'I thought I'd seen you here before. Weren't you a part of that group of students <u>what</u> used the gym lunchtimes?'

B 'That's right. I <u>see</u> you in there sometimes didn't I?'

A 'Yes. What was the sports therapy course like?'

B 'It was really good,'

A 'Did you have an induction for that course too?'

B 'Yes, it was different from this though. I remember we <u>was</u> split up into small groups and had to introduce each other to the whole class. I thought we would have done it in this class too.'

A 'Was that a bit nerve racking?'

B 'It <u>weren't</u> really nerve racking, although some of the students didn't have <u>nothing</u> to say so run off before it was their turn to speak. <u>Was</u> you here yesterday afternoon when we <u>done</u> that ice breaking exercise?'

A 'No I missed it.

Reading for understanding (14)

Read the passage below, and then answer the questions following:

Healthy Eating

Jamie Oliver's grand plan to convert the nation's schools to healthy eating habits got off to a flying start last night at the 'Make Britain Healthier' awards ceremony. Everyone agreed that the ceremony had been a success, and many people were eager to meet Oliver after the show, even if it was just for a brief moment, to ask the celebrity chef for his autograph.

The principal aim of his campaign is to persuade schools to provide meals that are balanced and healthy in order to do this, schools must ensure that their meals contain sufficient amounts of protein carbohydrates (including fibre) and fats, as well as a balance of vitamins and minerals. To achieve this, Oliver has suggested that a wide variety of menus are offered and that the ingredients used in the meals are fresh (i.e non-processed).

Although many say that his plans are good, others have questioned the cost of the plans and asked why children can't be allowed to decide for themselves what to eat. Nevertheless, studies have shown that children's behaviour does improve the healthier their diet becomes, and that if the meals are budgeted for correctly, the amount of money spent by schools on its dinners shouldn't rise.

Q. Match each of the following words below, with a word from the list that is similar in meaning:

enough - _____   principal - _____

rise - _____   eager - _____

fresh - _____   balanced - _____

sufficient, main, apparently, short, keen, expensive, decrease, encouraged, evenly distributed, non-processed, exterior, increase, persuaded

Q. List 4 things that a balanced diet should contain:

_____

Q. What was the name of the 'Awards Ceremony' in the above article?

_____

Q. Give one argument in favour of Jamie Oliver's plan:

_____

Q. Give one argument against Jamie Oliver's plan:

_____

Q. Write down one adjective used in the above passage.

_____

Q. Why does the word 'Oliver' have a capital letter?

_____

Q. There is a comma missing from the text. Place it in the correct position in the text.

Q. There is a full stop (followed by a capital letter) missing from the text. Place them in the correct position in the text.

Write 3 short sentences about your own diet (6):

_____

_____

Notes for tutor/vocational coach

Dictate six of the following sentences to the learner:

1. My friend got off the bus and walked to the centre of town.
2. The office managers were surprised to meet their targets in February.
3. She received an excellent prize for her dancing.
4. It doesn't matter too much if your planning application fails.
5. There will always be more chances here to exercise.
6. Please remember to come here earlier on Wednesday.
7. There were different families there yesterday.
8. We weren't allowed through the gates.
9. They went to the library to carry out some research.
10. The warm weather in February was quite unusual.

During the five minutes reading time, learners can be told or reminded of such things as:

- Remember to start each sentence with a capital letter and end it with a full stop (or question mark if it is a question).
- Capital letters should be used for I, days of the week, months of the year, place names, addresses, titles etc.
- For the grammar exercise, search for the verbs that look or sound wrong. If necessary, briefly outline the difference between a verb, noun and an adjective.

Marking

An answer sheet can be be provided. In the spelling exercise, two marks should be given for a correct sentence, and one mark if there is one mistake in the sentence. In the free writing exercise, two marks should be given for a correct sentence (i.e. with correct spelling, punctuation and grammar). If there are one or two errors in the sentence, then one mark should be given. If there are more than 2 errors, then no marks should be given. One mark can be given for legibility of the learner's writing.

After the assessment is marked, brief feedback (or as much feedback as the assessor feels comfortable with) can be given to the learner along with the answers. The learner then has the option of checking (and hence learning from) their assessment.

L2 Learning Assessment (Literacy)

Name: _____ **Date:** _____

The purpose of the assessment is to check any weak areas you may have, but more importantly to give you the chance to learn from it, and to develop everyday literacy skills. At the end of the assessment you can take away a copy of your paper together with an answer sheet to learn from.

Mark: ____   Level: ____
      40

Spelling (12)

Six sentences will be dictated to you by your tutor or vocational coach:

1. _____

2. _____

3. _____

4. _____

5. _____

6. _____

Grammar Exercise (7)

The following conversation between 2 people (A and B) contains some of the most common grammatical errors made in everyday spoken English. There are 8 errors in total. Underline each error and place the correct word above.

A   'Have you done any courses here before?'

B   'Yes, I done a sports therapy course here last year.'

A 'I thought I'd seen you here before. Weren't you a part of that group of students which used the gym lunchtimes?'

B 'That's right. I see you in there sometimes didn't I?'

A 'Yes. What was the sports therapy course like?'

B 'It was really good,'

A 'Did you have an induction for that course too?'

B 'Yes, it was different from this though. I remember we were split up into small groups and had to introduce each other to the whole class. I thought we would of done it in this class too.'

A 'Was that a bit nerve racking?'

B 'It wasn't really nerve racking, although some of the students ran off before it was their turn to speak. Were you here yesterday afternoon when we did that ice breaking exercise?'

A 'No I missed it. We came out of the library at about 2 o'clock, and by the time we got to the class it had finished. They give us some stuff to look at though, so I've got that.'

B 'Could you borrow me your notes later so I could photocopy them?'

A 'O.K. but will you call me when you've finished with them?'

B 'Sure, but I haven't got no credit left on my phone.'

A 'It don't matter, I'll collect them when I see you next.

Reading for understanding (15)

Read the passage below and then answer the following questions:

© Mark Bracey

BRONTE COUNTRY

Welcome to Bronte Country, an area which spans the West Yorkshire and East Lancashire Pennines in the North of England. A windswept land of heather and wild moors, it is hardly surprising that this region became the inspiration for the classic works of the Bronte sisters, Charlotte, Emily and Anne.

Bronte Country consists of the Pennine hills immediately to the west of (but also including) the cities of Bradford and Leeds in West Yorkshire. The geology in Bronte Country is predominantly dark sandstone, which gives the scenery a feeling of bleakness it is no surprise then, that this landscape fuelled the imagination of the Bronte sisters in writing their classic novels including "Wuthering Heights" and "Jane Eyre".

Most of the Bronte locations lie within easy reach of the village of Haworth, where the Bronte family lived at the Haworth parsonage (now the world famous Bronte Parsonage Museum), and where they wrote most of their famous works (including "Wuthering Heights" and "Jane Eyre" etc). Other Bronte related attractions in the heart of Bronte Country include the Bronte Birthplace in Thornton on the outskirts of Bradford (where Charlotte, Emily and Anne were born while their father was parson at Thornton church), and Ponden Hall near Haworth ("Thrushcross Grange" in "Wuthering Heights") and Oakwell Hall in Kirklees.

Other famous people associated with The Bronte Country include the playwright J.B. Priestley, the composer Delius, the novelist John Braine and the artist David Hockney, all of whom (like the Bronte sisters themselves) were born within the 40 district of the city of Bradford, and the poet Ted Hughes, who was born near Hebden Bridge.

Do you want to find out more. If you wish to access a full list of places to visit and practical information about Bronte Country, then please take a look at our list of books and other products about the Brontes (and Bronte Country). Alternatively, you can find more information on our website (www.bronte-country.com), including links to accommodation and where to eat etc.

Q. Match each of the following words below, with a word from the list that is similar in meaning:

scenery - _____

outskirts - _____

novelist - _____

predominantly - _____

spans - _____

bleakness - _____

interior, mainly, apparently, landscape, excellent, desolation, secondary, scenic, writer, painter, exterior, crosses, avoids, periphery, picturesque

Q. Where were the Bronte sisters born?

_____

Q. Where was 'Jane Eyre' written?

_____

Q. What name was given to Ponden Hall in Wuthering Heights?

_____

Q. Apart from the Bronte sisters, name two other writers associated with Bronte country:

_____

Q. Why do the words 'Wuthering Heights' contain capital letters?

_____

Q. There is a question mark missing from the text. Place it in the correct position in the text.

Q. There is a full stop (followed by a capital letter) missing from the text. Place them in the correct position in the text.

Q. The purpose of the image is to:
  A) Inform the reader of the attractions of Bronte country.
  B) Show the reader where the Pennine hills are located.
  C) Give the reader an impression of Bronte country.
  D) Show the reader the location of the village of Howarth.

Q. What is the main purpose of the article?

A) To inform the reader of the attractions of Bronte country.
B) To inform the reader where the Bronte sisters were born.
C) To inform the reader about the world famous Bronte Parsonage Museum.
D) To inform the reader of the geology of the landscape.

Free writing (6)

Write 50 – 60 words about a place you have visited recently, **or** about what you did in a previous job role:

_____

_____

_____

_____

_____

_____

_____

_____

_____

Notes for tutor/vocational coach

Dictate six of the following sentences to the learner:

1. I thought it wouldn't be necessary to liaise with my manager.
2. The advertisement received its first endorsement yesterday.
3. To become a professional, you need to have more than just the occasional practice session.
4. The atmosphere in my new accommodation wasn't great.
5. He said, 'We should have practised regularly.'
6. The children's bicycles had their first maintenance check yesterday.
7. The headmaster's secretary welcomed the new Health Commissioner.
8. He told everyone that he would make a significant announcement later in the day.
9. It appears that they are still fighting for independence or a separate homeland.
10. The privileged few were given a particularly hard time.

During the five minutes reading time, learners can be told or reminded of such things as:

- Remember to start each sentence with a capital letter and end it with a full stop (or question mark if it is a question).
- Capital letters should be used for I, days of the week, months of the year, place names, addresses, titles etc.
- For the grammar exercise, search for the verbs that look or sound wrong. If necessary, briefly outline the difference between a verb, noun and an adjective.

Marking

An answer sheet can be provided. In the spelling exercise, two marks should be given for a correct sentence, and one mark if there is one mistake in the sentence. In the free writing exercise, two marks should be given for a correct sentence (i.e. with correct spelling, punctuation and grammar). If there are one or two errors in the sentence, then one mark should be given. If there are more than 2 errors, then no marks should be given. One mark can be given for legibility of the learner's writing.

After the assessment is marked, brief feedback (or as much feedback as the assessor feels comfortable with) can be given to the learner along with the answers. The learner then has the option of checking (and hence learning from) their assessment.

Answers to L1 literacy learning assessment

Grammar (8)

A   'Have you done any courses here before?'

B   'Yes, I did a sports therapy course here last year.'

A   'I thought I'd seen you here before. Weren't you a part of that group of students **which** (or **that** or **who**) used the gym lunchtimes?'

B   'That's right. I **saw** you in there sometimes didn't I?'

A   'Yes. What was the sports therapy course like?'

B   'It was really good,'

A   'Did you have an induction for that course too?'

B   'Yes, it was different from this though. I remember we **were** split up into small groups and had to introduce each other to the whole class. I thought we would have done it in this class too.'

A   'Was that a bit nerve racking?'

B   'It **wasn't** really nerve racking, although some of the students didn't have **anything** to say so **ran** off before it was their turn to speak. **Were** you here yesterday afternoon when we **did** that ice breaking exercise?'

A   'No I missed it.

Reading for understanding (14)

Q. Match each of the following words below, with a word from the list that is similar in meaning:

enough - **sufficient**   rise - **increase**

fresh - **non-processed**   principal - **main**

eager - **keen**   balanced – **evenly distributed**

Q. List 4 things that a balanced diet should contain:
Four from; proteins, carbohydrates, fats, vitamins and minerals.

Q. What was the name of the 'Awards Ceremony' in the above article?
'Make Britain Healthier'

Give one argument in favour of Jamie Oliver's plan:
It could improve children's behaviour and/or health or children's school dinners would be healthier or similar answer.

Q. Give one argument against Jamie Oliver's plan:
Children should be allowed to decide for themselves or there could be an increase in costs if school dinners are made healthier or similar answer.

Q. Write down one adjective used in the above passage.
One of grand, healthy, eager, brief, principal, wide, fresh, good

Q. Why does the word 'Oliver' have a capital letter?
Because it is a person's name.

Q. There is a comma missing from the text. Place it in the correct position in the text:
…sufficient amounts of protein**,** carbohydrates (including fibre) and fats, …

Q. There is a full stop (followed by a capital letter) missing from the text. Place them in the correct position in the text:
…to provide meals that are balanced and healthy**. I**n order to do this, schools must …

Answers to L2 literacy learning assessment

Grammar (7)

A 'Have you done any courses here before?'

B 'Yes, I **did** a sports therapy course here last year.'

A 'I thought I'd seen you here before. Weren't you a part of that group of students which used the gym lunchtimes?'

B 'That's right. I **saw** you in there sometimes didn't I?'

A 'Yes. What was the sports therapy course like?'

B 'It was really good,'

A 'Did you have an induction for that course too?'

B 'Yes, it was different from this though. I remember we were split up into small groups and had to introduce each other to the whole class. I thought we would **have** done it in this class too.'

A 'Was that a bit nerve racking?'

B 'It wasn't really nerve racking, although some of the students ran off before it was their turn to speak. Were you here yesterday afternoon when we did that ice breaking exercise?'

A 'No I missed it. We came out of the library at about 2 o'clock, and by the time we got to the class it had finished. They **gave** us some stuff to look at though, so I've got that.'

B 'Could you **lend** me your notes later so I could photocopy them?'

A 'O.K. but will you call me when you've finished with them?'

B 'Sure, but I haven't got **any** credit left on my phone.'

A 'It **doesn't** matter, I'll collect them when I see you next.

Reading for understanding (15)

Q. Match each of the following words below, with a word from the list that is similar in meaning:

scenery - **landscape**   outskirts - **periphery**

novelist - **writer**   predominantly - **mainly**

spans - **crosses**   bleakness - **desolation**

Q. Where were the Bronte sisters born? **Thornton** or **Bradford**

Q. Where was 'Jane Eyre' written? **The Howarth parsonage**

Q. What name was given to Ponden Hall in Wuthering Heights?
Thorncrush Grange

Q. Apart from the Bronte sisters, name two other writers associated with Bronte country: Any two from **J B Priestly, John Braine and Ted Hughes**

Q. Why do the words 'Wuthering Heights' contain capital letters?
Because it's the name (or title) of a book or **because it's a place name**

Q. There is a question mark missing from the text. Place it in the correct position in the text.
Do you want to find out more**?**

Q. There is a full stop (followed by a capital letter) missing from the text. Place them in the correct position in the text.
Bronte Country consists of the Pennine hills immediately to the west of (but also including) the cities of Bradford and Leeds in West Yorkshire. The geology in Bronte Country is predominantly dark sandstone, which gives the scenery a feeling of bleakness. It is no surprise then, that this landscape fuelled the imagination of the Bronte sisters in writing their classic novels including "Wuthering Heights" and "Jane Eyre".

Q. The purpose of the image is to:
A) Inform the reader of the attractions of Bronte country.
B) Show the reader where the Pennine hills are located.
C) Give the reader an impression of Bronte country.
D) Show the reader the location of the village of Howarth.

Q. What is the main purpose of the article?

A) To inform the reader of the attractions of Bronte country.

B) To inform the reader where the Bronte sisters were born.

C) To inform the reader about the world famous Bronte Parsonage Museum.

D) To inform the reader of the geology of the landscape.

Spelling

Some spelling rules

Before trying the following exercises, you should be aware of the following spelling rules:

i and e

Put i before e, except after c, when the sound rhymes with bee.
Examples:

> piece, thief, belief, believe, hygiene, brief, priest, shield, relief, niece, pier, chief, ceiling, receive, receipt, deceive, conceive

However, there are some exceptions e.g. weird and seize

Also, be aware of words where e comes before i when the sound doesn't rhyme with bee e.g. height, weight, leisure, their

Making plural from nouns ending in y

If the letter immediately before the y is a consonant, change the y into i and add –es.
Examples:

> Penny – pennies   lorry - lorries   industry – industries   company – companies

If the letter immediately before the y is a vowel (a, e, i, o u) simply add s
Examples:

> Valley – valleys monkey – monkeys turkey – turkeys

Try remembering the spelling of the following commonly misspelled words. For each word, look at it, cover it, say it, write it out, and then check the spelling: careful, carefully, usual, usually, peaceful, peacefully, sudden, suddenly, occasion, occasional, occasionally, knife, knives, leaf, leaves, shelf, shelves, wife, wives, church, churches, brush, brushes, address, addresses, business, businesses, write, writing, make, making, notice, noticing, excite, exciting, (age, ageing), exercise, carry, carrying, carried, hurry, hurrying, hurried, shop, shopping, travel, travelling, trip, tripped, pass, passed, possess, possessed, necessary, separate, vegetable, different, difference, reference, interest, interesting, computer, mechanic, excellent, always, advertisement, professional, attached, assistant, earlier, surprise, foreign, responsible, responsibilities, Wednesday, February, tomorrow, through, necessary, beautiful, restaurant, early, earlier, science, argue, argument

Punctuation

Read the following information and try the punctuation exercise.

Capital letters are used at the beginning of a sentence, for days of the week (e.g. **W**ednesday) and months of the year (e.g. **F**ebruary), for the word **I**, for proper nouns (place names, people's names and names of countries, mountains and rivers), for addresses, for names of products and brand names (e.g. **W**alkers, **N**ike etc.), for names of festivals (e.g. **C**hristmas, **R**amadan etc), for names of nationalities (e.g. **E**nglish, **C**hinese etc) and for titles (e.g. **M**rs, **D**r etc).

Full stops (.) are placed at the end of sentences**.**

A **question mark (?)** is placed at the end of a sentence which asks a question.
e.g. How do you apply for a passport**?** Do you like sugar**?** Are you alright**?**
However, it is not placed after a statement e.g. How to apply**.**

Exclamation marks (!) are used at the end of a statement showing surprise or shock, or at the end of an order, exclamation or cry e.g. Don't look**!** I don't believe it**!**
The meaning of a sentence can be altered by changing the punctuation mark at the end. For example:
    They drove on the motorway.   –   Statement
    They drove on the motorway?   –   Question
    They drove on the motorway!   –   Exclamation (showing surprise or shock)

Commas (,) are used to mark a pause in a sentence, divide items in a list and to separate words from the rest of the sentence which gives information but is not vital to make sense. For example:
    I don't like jogging**,** but I enjoy swimming.
    We need carrots**,** eggs**,** a couple of loaves of bread**,** mushrooms and carrots.
    Next month**,** after we've finished our course**,** we'll start our Christmas shopping.

Apostrophes (')
An omissive **apostrophe** is used to replace a missing letter (or letters) when

two words are joined together. For example:

I **do not** know where they are = I **don't** know where they are

We have got six months left = **We've** got six months left

Possessive **apostrophes** are used to indicate that something belongs to someone or something. For example:

The boy's computer = The computer of the boy

The children's books = The books of the children

The lady's coat = The coat of the lady

Ladies' fashions = Fashions of the ladies

The boys' teams = The teams of the boys

In next week's episode = In the episode of next week

L1 Sentence examples

Read the following sentences, then practise writing them:

1. My friend got off the bus and walked to the centre of town.
2. The office managers were surprised to meet their targets.
3. She received an excellent prize for her dancing.
4. It doesn't matter too much if your planning application fails.
5. There will always be more chances here to exercise.
6. Please remember to come here earlier on Wednesday.
7. There were different families there yesterday.
8. We weren't allowed through the gates.
9. He wrote everything down carefully.
10. They went to the library to carry out some research.
11. The warm weather in February was quite unusual.
12. He was hoping to wear the suit that had been designed especially for him.
13. They would only go to the fair if they could go on their favourite rides.
14. The lorries drove quickly down the motorway.
15. She preferred writing at night, when the house was quiet.
16. They had to count their pennies before deciding to go on holiday.
17. Although she was quite old, her eyesight was still good.
18. We listened to the radio all day, but unfortunately our song wasn't played.
19. You need to be careful whilst driving on the right hand side of the road.
20. It was a suitable occasion to celebrate the people's success.
21. The children's books were stacked on the shelves.
22. Weren't you happy with the arrangements at the theatre?

From the above sentences, write down:

2 nouns	_____	_____
2 adjectives	_____	_____
2 verbs	_____	_____
2 adverbs	_____	_____

Literacy Exercise (a)

Read the following passage and make any corrections. There are ten errors to be found (spelling, punctuation and grammar):

The managers was surprised to here about the theft. They were told that the thieves had broken into the hotel and stolen there keys. They recieved the news quite late at night. They were told that the thieves had been give to much opportunities to break in.

Have you ever had something stolen.
If your'e planing to make your house more secure, you should do so instantaneously.

Literacy Exercise (b)

Read the following passage and make any corrections. There are 15 errors to be found (spelling, punctuation and grammar):

The new assesor, who come from the north of England started work for the new company last Friday throughout his first few days, he often asked himself why he'd come south to look for work in the first place. I heard him ask a coleague, Do you think life is so much better in the south"

"Not necessarilly" his colleague replied, "Don't decieve yourself" he continued, "ask for other peoples views but decide for yourself after youve lived here a while. There's a few clubs you could join to get to know some people. It don't really matter who you ask though, as everyones biased to some extent.

L2 Sentence examples

Read the following sentences, then practise writing them:

1. I thought it wouldn't be necessary to liaise with my manager.
2. The advertisement received its first endorsement yesterday.

3. To become a professional, you need to have more than just the occasional practice session.

4. The atmosphere in my new accommodation wasn't great.

5. He said, 'We should have practised regularly.'

6. The children's bicycles had their first maintenance check yesterday.

7. The headmaster's secretary welcomed the new ',successful Health Commissioner.

8. He told everyone that he would make a significant announcement later in the day.

9. It appears that they are still fighting for independence or a separate homeland.

10. The privileged few were given a particularly hard time.

11. The Government is clearly struggling in this current recession.

12. The effects of climate change are becoming clearly visible.

13. Jim felt quite embarrassed when he was informed, in front of the whole class, that he had successfully achieved his qualification.

14. Scientists are currently debating the degree to which climate change is affecting our environment.

15. Contingency plans were drawn up by the regional executive.

16. The train pulled away unexpectedly, while its international passengers slept.

17. The thermometer showed a rapid rise in temperature.

18. As a result of accumulating debts, he felt obliged to sell his collection of sports cars.

19. The more expensive items in her collection included jewellery, some antique furniture and a Persian rug.

20. The ambassador's residence was well furnished.

Capital Letters and Full Stops

Read the sentences below and place full stops and capital letters where they are needed:

1. i went to brighton last week and i'll go there again tomorrow

2. my friend likes to keep fit he eats healthily and goes swimming most days of the week

3. she took longer than expected to reach the border, because the coach kept stopping

4. harry and steve are flying to berlin in october they'll stay there for about a week, then travel across to britain

5. george felt unwell during the conference, so left before the end

6   i had bacon, eggs tomatoes, beans and mushrooms for breakfast, so for lunch i'll probably just have a tuna sandwich

7   he called the surgery to arrange a telephone appointment with one of the doctors dr john then called him sometime in the afternoon

8   there were lots of people at the party last night most of them were new to the organisation

9   they didn't really want to stay at the sheraton hotel, but at the end of the day they didn't really have much of a choice

10 there were twenty five students in the classroom, all of whom were waiting to do their assessment

11 for lunch we had fishcakes, rice and vegetables later we had bread and butter pudding for dessert

12 i'll never forget that adventure in lake Malawi it's hard to believe that we were stuck in the mud when the flash storm started

Apostrophes (to show belonging)

Underline the nouns in the following sentences. In terms of word classes, what is the rule governing the use of the possessive apostrophe?

_____

Place apostrophes in the correct position in the following sentences:
1. The assessors read through the learners portfolio.
2. The verifiers observed the assessors all afternoon.
3. I read the stories in last weeks newspapers.
4. He ran his familys business like anyone elses business.
5. My childrens ages are six and seven.
6. He was the peoples choice.
7. The mens room is just around the corner.
8. The dogs collar is red. It is wagging its tail.
9. He read his brothers book with great enthusiasm.
10. She receives her paycheques on a regular basis.

In the following sentences, underline the words which contain an apostrophe:
1. **!*!--) noun verb adverb -- !".:
2. **!*!--) adjective noun adjective noun -- !".:
3. **!*!--) noun noun verb adverb -- !".:
4. **!*!--) verb nouns adverb -- !".:

Look at these 4 sentences, then choose the correct answer below:

1. !!!"***… womens …,,!"**
2. "***,,,.. peoples --!!!!
3. ""!!::::: mens __---!1!1!!
4. $$£^^^** childrens ""!!!! ---

A) The apostrophe goes after the s in all of the above (s').
B) There is not enough information given to say where the apostrophe should go.
C) The apostrophe goes before the s in each of the above ('s).
D) There is no apostrophe in any of the above.

Punctuation Reading Exercises

Read the following passages and punctuate them in order that the text makes sense. Include capital letters, full stops, commas and apostrophes.
For commas, consider why they are used. For apostrophes, consider if they are possessive or omissive apostrophes. For possessive apostrophes, consider the noun-noun (or noun-adjective-noun) combination.

Exercise 1 (The Stockpot)

can i speak to the manager please i said rather nervously having just finished my meal

the restaurants location in londons west end combined with its friendly service and well-deserved reputation for serving reasonably priced food made it an ideal place for meeting up with friends before a show the menu offered mainly anglo european cuisine consisting of traditional dual composites such as liver and bacon fish and chips apple crumble and custard bubble and squeak and jelly and ice cream etc

sure ill tell him she replied

a minute or so later after finishing making some drinks from behind the tiny bar the manager walked the few yards across towards our table and gave me a slightly puzzled look id been there enough times for him to recognise me as a regular customer and for me to recognise him as one of the managers

ive been coming here and your other restaurants for the past thirty years i began in a precise deliberate tone designed perhaps to maintain the managers puzzled expression and have never had bad service i continued before pausing to maintain the suspense and i just wanted to say thank you

the manager remained perplexed for a moment or two before breaking into a cautious then more open smile

we like to do the best for our customers he eventually replied
thanks again i said feeling slightly awkward
youre welcome the manager replied

Exercise 2 (The midwife)

after the phone call the new midwife hastily put on her coat grabbed her well-worn leather bag of life delivery tools and following a long deep breath hurried out into the cold night air she then climbed onto one of the many midwives bicycles which were parked up against the wall of the nunnery and began cycling through the capital citys deserted streets of cobbled stones towards the nearby housing estate where an expectant mother and apprehensive father anxiously awaited

when she arrived the midwife climbed the grey grimy concrete steps to the familys home which was on the top floor of a block of flats throughout her first few days shed often asked herself why she'd taken up one of the most demanding jobs imaginable but three hours and one screaming baby later along with the look on the babys mothers face she realised that the midwifes job was a worthwhile one

Exercise 3 (The engineer)

dont forget latin America the tutor yelled as i made my way hurriedly from the classroom

i wont i replied slowing down with a feeling of guilt that i was rushing to get away

id wanted to stay after all during the break some in the group had suggested that as it was the last night of the latin american studies course we should all go out for a drink id made some good acquaintances on the course too i remember one of the guys from the group had asked me what my job was

im a civil engineer id said

I am a fugitive from a chain gang hed replied to my utter amazement hed seen the film on the telly the previous week he went on to say id seen it too but then I was a civil engineer and had waited for the film with excited anticipation as it was to my knowledge the only film until then that had been made about one it was a 1930s black and white Hollywood film about a civil engineer who as a wrongfully convicted convict on a chain gang puts up with intolerable conditions before escaping to chicago through his relationships his time on the chain gang come back to haunt him id seen it on a small portable black and white tv in a pokey little run down bedsit off the kings road in Fulham

Grammar Exercise

In the following passage, there are six grammatical errors. Underline and correct them.

The organisers could have run the project themselves. After all, it was their idea. However, most of them was probably too inexperienced, and couldn't have known everything that was involved in managing such a large project or how much it would cost.

Although the sports council had given plenty of money for similar ideas in the past, last year they only give a small amount towards their project. Following this, the organisers weren't able to get no equipment, and therefore many of the training sessions had to be cancelled. As a result, the clients stop coming to the centre and instead began using the facilities at the nearby business park. Problems then seemed to come their way from all directions. The organisers could have guessed what was likely to happen, but it wasn't until the letters started arriving in the post that they could finally saw the extent of their problems. When the director of the sports council actually come to see them at their office early one morning, they knew that their project was nearing the end of its time.

More or Less?

Look at this photograph of a typical sign above a checkout till that can be seen in many large supermarkets.

- Why is the sign not correct?

_____

_____

_____

_____

- If you're able to answer the above, then find a similar sign in a large supermarket and, by asking around, see if any members of the supermarket's staff (including managers) are aware of the error!

Discussion-based articles

The rationale behind the discussion-based articles, along with the Functional Skills reading and writing exercises is the belief that learners' literacy levels can be improved through increased engagement in society and that there is a clear correlation between people's general knowledge and cultural interests, and their literacy skills. As such, the main purpose of the following exercises is to encourage the reading of, and to develop an interest in, general topic and local interest articles through which general knowledge and vocabulary can be expanded, and spelling, grammar, punctuation and understanding of word classes improved. The articles chosen are of a general interest nature relating to areas such as education, diet, health, renewable energy, national and local news etc and come from a range of sources. Learners should be encouraged to bring into class articles of interest themselves from newspapers (local or national) or the internet.

Initially, students can either be asked to read to themselves or, depending on their reading ability, take it in turns to read out loud with a view to having their pronunciation checked and corrected as and when necessary. Following the reading of each article, and before the discussion, a range of questions relating to the vocabulary, expressions/figures of speech, spelling, punctuation features and grammar within the article can be asked, and discussed, depending on the abilities of the learners in the class. During the discussion-based articles, an 'integrated approach' is encouraged whereby a wider vocabulary, along with knowledge and understanding of word classes, punctuation features, and spelling, and how they are related, is promoted.

Article 1

'The more you have in a class, the harder the teacher's job is'

Liz Green is concerned that her three-year-old daughter, Poppy, will miss out on a place at a local primary school next year.

In the London borough of Kingston upon Thames, at least 10 of the 34 primary schools will have temporary classrooms by September.

Without them, they would not be able to squeeze in all the children aged four and five in the area, says Green, an MP's assistant and Liberal Democrat councillor.

She says her part of the borough, Surbiton, needs at least one new primary school: "Temporary classrooms are not sustainable: we need permanent ones."

Next month the borough will publish its long-term strategy on tackling the problem. Two years ago, she says, the number of children who applied to go to the primary school outstripped the number of places. Some of her friends say their children were in classes with more than 40 pupils.

"That worries me," Green says. "The more you have in a class, the harder the teacher's job is. It would be better to have an extra form."

Green, 39, is thinking not just of Poppy, who should be going to school in September next year, but also of Martha, who is one.

"We're equidistant from two good primary schools, which are half a mile to a mile away. I wouldn't want them to go to a school further away than that. You are looking at buses and cars then. I want to walk them to the school gates, as my mother did for me. It's about being part of the community."

It would be easier out of London, where competition for places is less fierce.

But Green is adamant that she will stay in Surbiton: "I don't think it will end up being a problem."

Green has heard that one year, one of her preferred primary schools chose half of its pupils not because of the distance they lived from the school, but because they had siblings there. "There's nothing you can do about that, I suppose."

Jessica Shepard

Leading on from the reading of the article:

- In pairs, or individually, underline any words you are not sure of, and check their meaning in the dictionary, or using the Thesaurus on your computer (examples may include: adamant, strategy, equidistant, siblings, sustainable etc.)

- Locate and practise the spellings of the following words and sentences. Some of them will be tested by a brief dictation:

  temporary, permanent, assistant, September, friend, earlier, competition, community, daughter, councillor, further, primary, applied, 'the borough will publish its long-term strategy', 'that worries me'.

- Locate four pairs of commas in the text. What is the purpose of a pair of commas?

- Locate the spelling of "it's" and "its" in the text. What do the two different spellings represent?

  _____

- Give an example below, from the text, of the use of the possessive apostrophe:

  _____

- Give an example below, from the text, of the use of the omissive apostrophe:

  _____

- Which word class do the words 'teacher', 'job', 'MP' and 'assistant' belong to?

  _____

- Point for class discussion: What are class sizes like in primary schools in your area? Such a discussion can then lead on to other related issues concerning primary schools, such as school starting age and curriculum content etc.

Article 2   *Reproduced with kind permission from Centre for Cities*

Half of all young people in cities without Maths and English GCSE A* to C

The report, 'Learning Curve: Schooling and skills for future jobs' from Centre for Cities, and sponsored by ICAEW, shows that between 2007 and 2010 an average of almost 50% of pupils in cities left the education system without A* to C grades in GCSE Maths and English.

This, the Centre argues, not only has implications for young people's futures but also directly impacts on the economies of the cities they live in because businesses do not have access to the pool of skills they need.

As policy makers seek to support growth and the UK's global economic competitiveness, this report highlights the need to ensure we have the skills base necessary to meets these aspirations in the long-term.

Most notably, there is an obvious correlation at city level between GCSE Maths and English attainment and youth unemployment. The research shows cities perform at a similar level when you measure performance of GCSE A* to C grades across all subjects, but strikingly there are huge disparities between cities when looking at pupils' performance in Maths and English.

The Centre argues that owing to a misalignment of incentives in the education system schools are currently encouraged to strive for their pupils to attain 5 A* to C grades, even if these grades are achieved in less academic subjects. This means that schools are responding to the demands of an accountability system which overlooks the importance of Maths and English.

Centre for Cities is urging the Government to go further in its current plans to reform school league tables to ensure that the education system is aligned with the needs of businesses. The Centre holds that much greater weight should be attached to Maths and English attainment when measuring school performance in order to incentivise schools to focus on these core subjects. The Centre is also calling for the Pupil Premium to be used by local education authorities in struggling cities to help teachers that have the difficult job of helping their pupils to attain qualifications in Maths and English, to do so.

Summary of recommendations

- Greater emphasis should be placed on Maths and English attainment, particularly in struggling cities
- Publicly funded adult education and training should be targeted towards improving core skills amongst low skilled, disadvantaged groups
- As business-driven organisations, Local Enterprise Partnerships (LEPs) should work with skills providers and employers to improve access to adult education and training
- LEPs should work with employers and skills providers within the LEP area to increase employer demand for job-related training

For further information and to view the report, visit *www.centreforcities.org*

Leading on from the reading then:

- In pairs, or individually, underline any words you are not sure of, and check their meaning in the dictionary, or using the Thesaurus on your computer (examples may include: implications, disparities, correlation, aspirations etc.)

- Locate and practise the spellings of the following words and sentences. Some of them will be tested by a brief dictation:
economies, businesses, because, highlights, performance, unemployment, encouraged, academic, responding, accountability, importance, Government, attached, league, education, aligned, authorities, qualifications, difficult, emphasis, attainment, particularly, struggling, cities, publicly, employers, disadvantaged, access, increase, '… young people's futures …', '…when looking at pupils' performance …'.

- Look at the use of the apostrophe in the above two sentences. Why is the apostrophe placed before the 's' in people's?

_____

- Would the apostrophe ever be placed after the 's' (peoples')? What other words fall into this category (clue: see multiple choice question on p62).

_____

- Within the text, on the third paragraph, it states, 'As policy makers seek to support growth …' there is no apostrophe in the word 'makers'. Why not?

_____

- Which word class do the words 'people', 'future', 'pupils' and 'performance', used in the above article, belong to?

_____

- Which word class does the word 'young' belong to?

_____

- Which word class does the word 'highlights' (used in the third paragraph) belong to?

_____

- Point for class discussion: What are GCSE results like in secondary schools in your area? Such a discussion can then lead on to other related issues concerning secondary schools, such as education standards in general and the school leaving age etc.

Article 3

Morrisons forced to retrain school-leavers

The standard of school-leavers is so poor that one supermarket has sent back three-quarters of its recruits for "remedial pre-job training" before they start work.

Photo: ALAMY

Britain's fourth biggest supermarket, with 135,000 employees, found that many of its applicants in Salford, Greater Manchester, lacked even the basic skills needed to stack shelves and serve customers. While some had a poor grasp of maths and English, others lacked simple skills such as turning up on time and making eye contact.

The human resources director of the supermarket said, "Many of the people were just not job ready. They lacked a lot of confidence and social skills. It is quite clear the education system has failed them. Whatever the environment has been at school, it has not been conducive to instilling basic skills. It is a crying shame."

The warning will fuel concerns that schools are failing to teach the skills necessary for young Britons to find jobs, forcing firms to recruit migrant workers instead. The number of unemployed 16-to-24-year-olds now stands above one million, with one in five people in the age group now categorised as "Neets" – not in education, employment or training.

When the supermarket drew up plans for a new store in the employment black spot of Ordsall, Salford, it promised to give jobs to local youngsters. Of the 210 staff who will start work when the store opens, half left school with not a single GCSE to their name.

The supermarket sent back 150 of them for three to six months of remedial training including refresher courses in literacy and numeracy.

Some learnt customer service skills at Salford College while others were sent to Create, a social enterprise where "excluded" individuals practice working in a not-for-profit café and call centre.

Garry Stott, the chairman of Create, said, "Can these people read? Yes, they can. Can they write? That's more of a challenge. With maths most people have the basic skills but they struggle with the confidence to use it."

He said the main problem was school-leavers whose parents and grandparents who had never worked and lacked the aspiration to work. He added: "It is too simple to say it is because of the failure of the education system. It's more complex than that. But when I left school, many of my contemporaries were kicked out of the door on Monday morning by their Mum and Dad and told to go to work. For whatever reason that is not happening."

Government figures show that in 2.5 per

cent of households in north-west England, no adult has ever worked – the highest in the country after inner London. The supermarket is not the first major employer to lament the standards of school-leavers. Sir Terry Leahy, the former chief executive of Tesco, the country's largest private employer, said two years ago: "Sadly, despite all the money that has been spent, standards are still woefully low in too many schools. Employers like us are often left to pick up the pieces."

A survey of big employers six weeks ago found that thousands of young people arrive at interviews without the "vital employability skills" required by employers such as a suitable grasp of English, punctuality and a "can do" attitude.

Leading on from the reading then:

- In pairs, or individually, underline any words you are not sure of, and check their meaning in the dictionary, or using the Thesaurus on your computer (examples may include: remedial, conducive, instilling, contemporaries, lament, woefully etc.)

- Locate and practise the spellings of the following words. Some of them will be tested by a brief dictation:
employees, customers, shelves, applicant, grasp, resources, confidence, necessary, crying, education, recruit, environment, migrant, unemployed, million, categorised, promised, youngsters, tomorrow, literacy, individuals, enterprise, excluded, aspiration, households, highest, suitable, punctuality.

- How many pairs of commas are there in the second paragraph? What is their function?

  _____

- What is the function of the comma used in the fourth paragraph, after the word 'jobs,' on the second line?

  _____

- What is the function of the comma used in the fourth paragraph, after the word 'education,' on the fourth line?

  _____

- In the third paragraph, first line, why is a capital letter used in the word 'Many'?

  _____

- In the sixth paragraph, there is a spelling mistake. Can you spot it?

  _____

Use the word to complete the following table:

Noun	Verb
	To advise
licence	

Write three pairs of sentences, using one of the nouns or verbs from the above table in each sentence.

1. _____

   _____

2. _____

   _____

3. _____

   _____

   _____

In groups of 3 or 4, discuss the issue of 'Finding a job in today's economic climate'. In the discussion, reflect on your own experiences in trying to find work and/or that of people you know. Consider the points made in 'Holding a discussion – Good Practice' on p.110.

Article 4

Tweet victory for Trevor campaign

by Hayley O'Keeffe

hayley.okeeffe@jpress.co.uk

A TWITTER campaign to save a proud Bedford son from "peeing into the Christmas tree" has worked.

Bloggers Caroline Wise and Sue Gough, of Bedford Network, remarked online how a bust of the anti-apartheid campaigner Trevor Huddleston was being swamped by the newly erected Christmas tree in Silver Street.

The pair then launched a Twitter campaign which is gathering speed with many users lobbying the Mayor of Bedford, Dave Hodgson who has now announced that the tree location will be moved next year.

Caroline said: "It's a real shame to see Trevor being treated in this way.

"In our blog we write about the very best of Bedford and we think Trevor Huddleston is one of the best people who ever lived in Bedford, he campaigned all of his life for freedom and now his bust is being obscured.

NOT GOOD ENOUGH: Sue Gough and Caroline Wise with Trevor

"He is an inspiration to thousands of people and now he looks like he is peeing into the Christmas tree, it is very disrespectful."

In the year 2000 Huddleston's contribution was recognised by Nelson Mandela on his visit to Bedford where he unveiled the bust saying: "No white person has done more for South Africa than Trevor Huddleston."

Dave Hodgson, the Mayor of Bedford, said: "This year, we've trimmed back the branches to make the bust more visible. Next year, the pit will be moved to enable the tree to be placed in a more appropriate position.

"Christmas is a crucial time for the town centre, and I hope the lights and decorations will help encourage people to come and enjoy shopping in Bedford during the run-up to the festive season."

What's your view? Email us: editorial@timesandcitizen.co.uk

- In pairs, or individually, underline any words you are not sure of, and check their meaning in the dictionary, or using the Thesaurus on your computer (examples may include: obscure, unveil, lobbying, crucial, blog, blogger etc.)

- Locate and practise the spellings of the following words. Some of them will be tested by a brief dictation:
  campaigner, remarked, anti-apartheid, Christmas, swamped, freedom, inspiration, thousands, disrespectful, Mayor, trimmed, visible, appropriate, position, decorations, encourage, festive, season.

- Why has the writer placed the expression "peeing into the Christmas tree" in inverted commas?

- In the article it states, 'In the year 2000 Huddleston's contribution …'. What type of words are 'Huddleston' and 'contribution'?

  _____

- Rearrange the words 'Huddleston's contribution' to show why a possessive apostrophe has been used.

  _____

Points for class discussion: The words 'Twitter', 'Blogger', 'blog' etc. mentioned in the text are quite new to the English language. What are these words connected with? Can you think of other words which would come under the same category?

As the article states, Trevor Huddleston was from Bedford. Are there any famous (or infamous!) people from your home town? Why are they famous (or infamous)?

- Prepare a presentation (4 – 5 minutes) on a famous person that you admire. Consider the points made in 'For a successful presentation:' on p.110.
  Make notes on the lines below:

  _____

  _____

  _____

  _____

  _____

  _____

  _____

  _____

  _____

  _____

  _____

  _____

  _____

- On the lines below, write a short newspaper article about an event that has taken place in your local community recently. Include a heading to 'grab' the readers' attention.:

_____

_____

_____

_____

_____

_____

_____

_____

_____

_____

_____

_____

_____

_____

_____

_____

_____

_____

_____

_____

_____

_____

Article 5   *Reproduced with kind permission from www.midwintertuition.co.uk*

Elocution Basics *by Pauline Midwinter*

The importance of speaking correctly is becoming ever more relevant in this day and age. With conference calls and webcam meetings becoming more popular, clarity and diction are a must.

If you have an accent you can still speak clearly and in a manner which other people can understand you, even if you do not feel confident about it.

When I was training (at my BA (Hons) in Performing Arts (Suffolk College)) I was lucky enough to be vocally trained by a great man. Brian Theodore Ralph was a magnificent voice teacher and his booming voice ringing out across the classroom was an excellent example for us to attempt to emulate. Now, when I tutor people in elocution,
I aim to be the best example to them that I can, in honour of Brian!

In one of his lessons he told us to keep hold of our vocal training worksheets as 'we would need them some day.' I did not believe him but tucked them away and now I use them all the time! The basic principles he taught us are my ethos behind teaching elocution to my students.

Firstly I teach them how to understand their voice, both as part of their body and as a separate entity.

Secondly we learn how to enunciate vowel sounds in many different forms.

Next we add consonants to the vowels, not necessarily making real words but making sounds that sound like real words.

Once we have that sussed we move onto tongue twisters – not too quickly! We always try and work on them slowly at first to ensure accuracy, and then we speed them up when we are more confident.

The next thing I like to do is read poetry aloud. I find poetry with its nuances, rhythm and rhyme a pleasure to hear my students read and they gain a great deal of satisfaction from it too. We repeatedly read the same poem over and over until they and I are happy with the sound. I then encourage a 'performance reading' with all bells and whistles to finish.

All of this can be achieved with one hour's elocution tutoring! Then comes the tough part … implementing it in your everyday life.

Most people find it unnatural at first and do not feel confident enough to try out their 'new voice'. This then means they practise less and the effect of the tutoring wears off. I often get despondent with second lesson students! My message is to practise, practise, then practise some more. Even if your friends and family do not immediately notice it, they will!   **www.midwintertuition.co.uk**

- In pairs, or individually, underline any words you are not sure of, and check their meaning in the dictionary, or using the Thesaurus on your computer (examples may include: emulate, nuances, ethos, despondent, enunciate, sussed, entity etc.)

- Locate and practise the spellings of the following words and sentences. Some of them will be tested by a brief dictation:

importance, correctly, relevant, conference, popular, clarity, confident, accent, magnificent, voice, elocution, honour, worksheets, believe, excellent, example, separate, tongue, different, ensure, accuracy, pleasure, rhythm, rhyme, satisfaction, repeatedly, encourage, unnatural, friends, immediately, notice, 'The basic principles he taught us …', 'The next thing I like to do is read poetry aloud', 'This then means they practise less and the effect of the tutoring wears off'.

- Look at the ninth paragraph, beginning 'The next thing …' and complete the table below by identifying:

Two nouns:	
Two adjectives:	
Two conjunctions:	
Two verbs:	
Two adverbs:	
Two pronouns:	

- Points for class discussion: Do you think it would be a good idea to introduce elocution lessons into schools? Do you think there is a correlation between children's academic ability (and chances of going on to higher education and obtaining a good job etc) and the way they speak?

Article 6

One in five school leavers can't read

ONE in five school-leavers struggles to read and write because teachers are shunning traditional classroom methods in favour of trendy 'child-led' lessons, a report warns today.

Discredited teaching techniques that encourage children to just find things out for themselves rather than being taught are 'alive and kicking' in primary schools, the research claims. Teachers are encouraged to avoid pointing out mistakes for fear of 'crushing creativity' or 'undermining confidence', and to give pupils a choice of tasks to undertake in class. But the approach, typical of the 1960s and 1970s, is 'neither stimulating nor challenging' and is continuing to damage children's reading skills despite attempts by successive governments to introduce more structured teaching methods, according to the Centre for Policy Studies.

The report by Miriam Gross, a literary editor and volunteer teacher, warns that large sections of the educational establishment have ignored attempts to put traditional 'synthetic phonics' at the heart of reading lessons.

The technique involves children learning the 44 sounds of the English language and how they can be blended together to form words. But many teachers condemn it as 'prescriptive' and 'boring'. Instead, schools continue to use other, more 'fun', techniques, including encouraging children simply to memorise whole words and guess at harder ones.

The report, commissioned by Mayor of London Boris Johnson, highlights that more than a third of children who leave the capital's state primaries at 11 still have difficulties with reading, while one in five teenagers leave secondary school unable to read or write with confidence.

A separate study, by experts at Sheffield University, has found that 17 per cent of 16 to 19 year olds across the country are functionally illiterate meaning they can understand only the simplest text.

"This is less than the functional literacy needed to partake fully in employment, family life and citizenship and to enjoy reading for its own sake', the authors said.

Today's report warns that 'progressive' education theories still persist in many schools, damaging the prospects of thousands of children.

Teaching mixed ability classes is widespread, competition discouraged and mistakes of grammar, punctuation and spelling are too often left uncorrected.

Teachers are encouraged not to interrupt children while they are speaking or to pressure them into learning topics they don't like.

Unlike in other European countries, children are allowed to write in 'street' slang and teachers fail to point out how it differs from correct English usage for fear of stifling 'self-expression.'

'The child-led approach is frequently neither stimulating nor challenging. Very young children simply haven't got the tools or the knowledge to benefit from it or to make sensible choices', the report said. 'Disciplined learning and enjoyment are not mutually exclusive.'

At the same time, too much attention in primary schools is devoted to 'circle time', where children sit in a circle discussing emotions and family relationships.'

The report said: 'The great majority of children, at any rate under the age of eight or nine, are neither ready for nor interested in discussions about emotions, backgrounds and relationships.'

The study highlights examples of schools which have achieved outstanding results by shunning the 'do it yourself' approach and embracing more structured and rigorous teaching regimes.

The low literacy levels cannot be attributed to immigration, the report said, adding that children who don't speak English at home are often the most keen to learn.

The report recommends a new Booker prize-style literacy competition for primary schools to drive up standards. Schools would be independently assessed for their reading teaching and the best given a cash award.

- In pairs, or individually, underline any words you are not sure of, and check their meaning in the dictionary, or using the Thesaurus on your computer (examples may include: shunning, mutually, discredited, prescriptive, commissioned etc.)

- Locate and practise the spellings of the following words and sentence. Some of them will be tested by a brief dictation:
Traditional, undermining, confidence, approach, typical, stimulating, literary, editor, volunteer, creativity, successive, condemn, techniques, encouraging, memories, guess, difficulties, functionally, illiterate, separate, citizenship, progressive, persist, pressure, frequently, knowledge, disciplined,

relationships, majority, enjoyment, recommends, independently, 'continuing to damage children's reading skills'

• According to the article, what are people who are functionally illiterate excluded from?

_____

• In the second paragraph, why has the writer placed the words 'alive and kicking' in inverted commas?

_____

How many pairs of commas can you find in the text?

• Points for class discussion: Do you think that mixed ability classes are a good idea? What are the potential advantages and/or disadvantages? Do they have mixed ability classes in your local schools? What do you think are the main factors relating to low literacy standards in some schools, and in society in general?

• In groups of 3 or 4, discuss the issue of 'Standards in Education'. In the discussion, reflect on your own experiences at school. Consider the points made in 'Holding a discussion – Good Practice' on p.110.

Make notes in the space below:

Article 7

Obese adding to climate crisis

HIGH RATES OF OBESITY in richer countries cause up to 1billion extra tonnes of greenhouse gas emissions every year, compared with countries with leaner populations, according to a study that assesses the additional food and fuel requirements of the overweight. The finding is particularly worrying, scientists say, because obesity is on the rise in many rich nations.

"Population fatness has an environmental impact," said Phil Edwards, from the London School of Hygiene and Tropical Medicine. "We're all being told to stay fit and keep our weight down because it's good for our health. The important thing is that staying slim is good for your health and for the health of the planet."

The study, carried out by Edwards and Ian Roberts, is published today in the International Journal of Epidemiology.

In their model, the researchers compared a population of 1 billion lea people, with weight distributions equivalent to a country such as Vietnam, with 1 billion people from richer countries, such as the US, where about 40% of the population is classified obese.

The fatter population needed 19% more food energy for its energy requirements, they found. They also factored in greater car use by the overweight. "The heavier our bodies become the harder it is to move about in them and the more dependent we become on cars," they wrote.

The greenhouse gas emissions from food production and car travel for the fatter billion people were estimated at between 0.4 and 1 billion extra tonnes a year. That is a significant amount in comparison with the world's total emissions of 27 billion tonnes in 2004.

Last September the world's leading authority on climate change suggested that people should eat less meat, because meat production causes 20% of global emissions. Rajendra Pachauri, chairman of the UN Intergovernmental Panel on Climate Change, said consumers should begin with one meat-free day a week.

- In pairs, or individually, underline any words you are not sure of, and check their meaning in the dictionary, or using the Thesaurus on your computer (examples may include: epidemiology, Intergovernmental, emissions, consumer, leaner etc.)

- Locate and practise the spellings of the following words. Some of them will be tested by a brief dictation:
obesity, greenhouse, population, according, particularly, authority, significant, tropical, an environmental impact, international, researchers, population, classified, overweight, heavier, requirements, dependent,

estimated, suggested, comparison, production, September, climate change, consumers

- Look at the second paragraph. Name the punctuation marks used in the paragraph.

_____

Why does 'London School of Hygiene and Tropical Medicine' have capital letters?

_____

- Complete the following table:

Noun	Verb
production	
	To emit
distribution	
	To discuss
population	

- Points for class discussion: Are there any vegetarians in the class? What are the advantages and disadvantages of being a vegetarian?

- In groups of 3 or 4, discuss the issue of 'The effects of climate change.' Consider the points made in 'Holding a discussion – Good Practice' on p.110. Make notes in the space below:

- Prepare a presentation (4–5 minutes) on the importance of a healthy diet. Read documents 1 and 2 on pages 120–124. Consider the points made in 'For a successful presentation:' on p.110. Make notes on the lines below:

_____

_____

_____

_____

_____

_____

_____

_____

_____

_____

_____

_____

_____

_____

_____

_____

_____

_____

_____

_____

_____

_____

_____

Article 8

CAMELS: ONE HUMP OR TWO?

The Bactrian camel   The Arabian (or dromedary) camel

Domesticated thousands of years ago by traders, who trained the gangly cud-chewer to make the long and arduous journey from southern Arabia to the northern regions of the Middle East, the camel went on to become the desert dweller's primary source of transport, shade, milk, meat, wool and hides.

Two closely related types of camel are sometimes confused: the Arabian (or dromedary) camel with 1 hump and the Bactrian camel with 2 humps. The one-humped camel (Camelus dromedarius) is found in the very hot deserts of North Africa and the Middle East, while the two-humped camel (Camelus bactrianus) is found in the rocky deserts and steppes of Asia that get very hot and very cold. While Arabian camels are now all domesticated, some Bactrian camels still live in the wild in the Gobi desert, between southwest Mongolia and northwest China. Camels are well adapted to desert life and can go without food and water for 3 to 4 days:

THE HUMP

The camel's hump rises about 75cm (30 in) out of its body and contains fat (and NOT water). It stores up to 80 pounds (36 kilograms) of it, which the camel can break down into water and energy when sustenance is not available. These humps give camels their legendary ability to travel up to 100 desert miles (161 kilometers) without water.

ANATOMY

Camels are very strong mammals with wide, padded feet to help them navigate the rough, rocky terrain and shifting desert sands. They have thick leathery pads on their knees and chest to protect them from the hot desert sand when they kneel. Camels have nostrils that can close to keep sand at bay, and bushy eyebrows and two rows of long eyelashes protect their eyes from the sand. Their mouth is extremely tough, allowing them to eat thorny desert plants. Camels' ears are covered with hair, even on the inside. The hair helps keep out sand or dust that might blow into the animal's ears. The colour of their bodies helps them to blend into their environment.

WATER AND TEMPERATURE

Unlike most mammals, a healthy camel's body temperature fluctuates throughout the day from 34°C to 41.7°C (93°F-107°F). This allows the camel to conserve water by not sweating, even in desert temperatures that reach 120°F (49°C), so when they do take in fluids they can conserve them for long periods of time. In winter, even desert plants may hold enough moisture to allow a camel to live without water for several weeks. When they do refill, however, they soak up water like a sponge. A very thirsty camel can drink 30 gallons (135 litres) of water in only 13 minutes.

DIET:

Camels are herbivores (plant-eaters). Most camels are domesticated and are fed by people; they eat dates, grasses, wheat, herbs, leaves and oats.

OTHER FACTS ABOUT CAMELS:

Camels have long been valued as pack animals. They can carry large loads for up to 25 miles (40 kilometers) a day. A camel can run up to 40 miles per hour (mph) in short bursts and sustain speeds of up to 25 mph. The average life expectancy of a camel is 40 to 50 years. A fully grown adult camel stands 1.85 m (6ft 1in) at the shoulder and 2.15m (7ft 1 in) at the hump, and weighs in excess of 1,600 pounds (725 kg).

....

- Describe what the following words mean, and state whether they are nouns, verbs or adjectives:

  Arduos _____

  Steppes _____

  Terrain _____

  Fluctuate _____

  Sustenance _____

  Legendary _____

  Anatomy _____

- Which of the two types of camel is not entirely domesticated?

  _____

- It states in the text that 'camels are herbivores (plant-eaters).'
  What are we?

  _____

- The phrase, "The straw that broke the camel's back" is a well-known English idiom. What does it mean?

  _____

  What do the following well-known idioms mean?

  "The last straw"   _____

  "Donkeys' years"   _____

  "Safe as houses"   _____

  "The writing is on the wall" _____

  "Breaking the ice"   _____

  "Back to square one"   _____

  "Double whammy"   _____

  "Saved by the bell"   _____

- On the lines below, write about an animal that you liked as a child. Give as many details as you can about the animal, including its scientific name, and explain why you liked it:

  _____

  _____

  _____

  _____

  _____

  _____

  _____

  _____

  _____

  _____

  _____

  _____

  _____

  _____

- The article states that the camel was 'the desert dweller's primary source of transport. In groups of 3 or 4, discuss what local transport, and traffic, is like in your area. Consider the points made in 'Holding a discussion – Good Practice' on p.110 Make notes in the space below:

Article 9

Kayaking is the use of a kayak for moving across water. Kayaking and canoeing are also known as paddling. Kayaking is generally differentiated from canoeing by the sitting position of the paddler and the number of blades on the paddle.

There are many types of kayak one can use, depending on what type of water you are on:

Sea kayak

Sea kayaking is where you paddle along the sea in a long, thin kayak that sits high in the water. They can be as long as 10–18ft and can be used for long periods of time as they have the facilities to hold lots of cargo, such as water and food.

Play boat

Play boating is a discipline of white-water kayaking where the paddler performs various technical moves in one place (a play spot) as opposed to downriver white-water kayaking where the objective is to travel the length of a section of river. Play boats are typically less than 10 ft long and are made for freestyle play or competition. The design of a play boat, usually a blunted bow and stern with a flattened hull, enables the kayaker to perform stunts such as vertical spins and airborne tricks, similar to those performed by snowboarders, surfers or skaters.

River Waves

There is a fair amount of science behind how river waves are formed and work. Put simply however, they are formed by a sudden increase in river depth. This causes the water to form standing waves that can be surfed. To stay on the wave, the kayaker relies on balancing the gravity pulling them down the face of the wave and the water pushing them downstream. The act of surfing on river waves is very similar to surfing a sea wave.

- Which parts of a boat do the following represent?

  a) The bow _____

  b) The stern _____

  c) The hull _____

- On the lines below, write a short story about a sport or game you enjoyed playing when you were younger:

_____

_____

_____

_____

_____

_____

_____

_____

_____

_____

_____

_____

_____

_____

_____

_____

_____

_____

_____

_____

_____

_____

_____

_____

_____

- Prepare a presentation (4–5 minutes) on a hobby or interest that you have. Consider the points made in 'For a successful presentation:' on p.110. Make notes in the space below:

Article 10

An African Story

WE SPENT SOME OF THE REST OF THE DAY exploring the capital, Lilongwe, before heading back to the tobacco farm. The plan was to leave Lilongwe the following morning and head down towards a village near Zomba (in the south of the country, not far from Blantyre, Malawi's second largest city and centre of finance and commerce) on the basis that Phiri had been informed that there were relatives of his father still living there who would have remembered him as a young boy. However, we decided to leave that evening, partly to avoid putting upon and inconveniencing our guests, and partly due to the fact that I believed some expat colleagues of mine would be staying at one of the guest houses on Monkey Bay, in the southern region of Lake Malawi, within the tourist Cape McClear Nature Reserve and I wanted to meet up with them.

We didn't end up leaving Lilongwe until after dark, but that didn't seem to matter, as it didn't appear to be a huge distance to travel. En route towards the lake however, not far from a town we passed through called Dedza, which happened to be the highest town in Malawi, the road turned into a construction site and just prior to it, we came off on a detour. We followed the detour for a couple of miles on an untarmaced, yet fairly compact dirt track, which ran more or less adjacent to the road construction site, then something didn't seem to feel right. The night had become as dark as coal as we approached a fork in the road. The left side, which seemed like a natural progression of the dirt track appeared blocked with fallen or purposefully placed branches and wooden debris, so I took the fork to the right, which led us down the slope of a much less firm dirt track until, before I realised what was happening, the Sentra ran aground in the squelchy mire at the bottom!

I tried in vain to get the car moving again, but alas, the required traction wasn't forthcoming. We both got out of the car, placed any solid objects we could find, mainly branches, beneath the tyres, and started heaving. It was in vain though, as the Sentra refused to budge under our combined and varied efforts. A feeling of minor dread hit me as I realised that we would not only fail to to get our planned destination that night, but that we'd be stuck in the mud for some time to come. There didn't seem a lot of choice as to what to do next, stay in the car, chat and sleep off the misfortune until daybreak. And talk we did, but the frustration of getting stranded in the middle of somewhere, seemed to stifle our usual, more energetic level of conversation. After a while though, the talking stopped, the seats went back as far as they could and attempts were made to find as comfortable a position as possible in order to drift off. The limited space and comfort on the inside of the Sentra though made this difficult, allowing a mixture of old and new unconstructive thoughts to come to the surface of my mind, rehash themselves, linger and refuse to filter to my sub-consciousness.

The first drops of rain spluttering on the surface of the Sentra helped to knock some of those thoughts out of place, but after a matter of minutes when they developed into a storm, hammering to break into the car, they became a focus in themselves, a centre of gravity for them. I remembered the flash storm during my first day at Moshupa Secondary School just after meeting Harry, and then reflected on the fact that through him (and his friendship with Phiri), I was in another one near Lake Malawi.

As the storm continued, I became more and more drowsy, drifting in and out through various stages of consciousness. After some time I was shaken out of one of its lower levels when I heard, and sensed, Phiri sit up with a sudden jolt! As I glanced across, barely awake, I saw him staring out of the window. The sound of the rain came back into my ears to confirm the continuation of the storm, and as it did so I looked out of the window too to see what Phiri was looking at.

In the conscious time between the knowledge that pain is going to come (like after touching something hot or cutting yourself), and the pain itself, there's a cold, fuzzy, slightly distressing, distraught, sinking realisation that something has to be done, physical movement has to be made against a force and desire to stay and wish that you could go back to however it was that split second ago. When the moment had passed, there was no time for further thought, reflection or utterances, only movement leading to us getting the hell out of the car as fast as humanly possible! With that in mind, and by now as alert and as focussed as I could be within such a short space of time, Phiri and I forced our doors open in sync allowing a few inches of water to come flooding in, but more importantly, allowing us to get out, wade through to the boot of the car, open it up, grab our rucksacks and continue wading out of the water until what we came to realise later was the riverbank!

At that point, we spotted nearby approaching bright, dazzling lights between the trees coming along an apparent ridge on a near invisible horizon, so continued worked our way up through the sludge shouting instinctively as we did, with whatever spare air we had left in our lungs. As we scrambled up the side of the embankment, like a couple of drowning rats, we noticed that the lights had come to a halt, and we began to make out the outline of a pick-up truck.

"What were the chances of that?" I thought to myself, "Then what are the chances of anything?" I continued to reflect.

As we hastily came within reach of the truck, the driver wound down his window and shouted:

"Was that you in the car stuck in the river bed?"

"Yes, I'm afraid so" Phiri shouted back, as if the sound of a loud voice was needed to confirm that we were still living through the experience. The sight of the truck and its driver was as welcome as rain in the dessert.

"Any chance of a lift to anywhere, like a rest house or something?" I followed on, desperate to confirm an escape route from the nightmare.

"Sure, get in the back" the driver responded, "There's a rest house just a few miles away."

So, we lobbed our rucksacks into the back, quickly followed by our greatly relieved, and just about nimble enough, selves, but not before looking back in almost total disbelief as the last few visible inches of my beloved Sentra faded away into the abyss. © Kevin Norley

- Describe what the following words mean, and state whether they are nouns, verbs or adjectives:

  Expat - _____

  Squelchy - _____

  Mire - _____

Debris - _____

Traction - _____

Adjacent - _____

Utterance - _____

Distraught - _____

Ridge - _____

Lob - _____

Abyss - _____

- The expression 'en route' used in the second paragraph comes from the French language, but is commonly used in English. What does it mean?

_____

- What do the following commonly used French expressions mean?

Bonne Voyage _____

Déjà vu _____

Bonne appetite _____

Après ski _____

Faux pas _____

Rendezvous _____

C'est la vie _____

Raison d'être _____

Tête a tête _____

Double entendre _____

Touché _____

- Similes and Metaphors

A **simile** is where two things are directly compared because they are alike in some regard. The word 'as' or 'like' is used to compare the two things. For example, in the text above, 'The night had become **as** dark **as** coal' and 'we scrambled up the side of the embankment **like** a couple of drowning rats' are similes.

A **metaphor** is a nonliteral or figurative expression where something is written or spoken in terms usually associated with something else. For example, in the text above, '**A feeling of minor dread hit me**' is a metaphor.

Can you find another example of a simile in the above text?

_____

On the lines below, give two examples of similes and two examples of metaphors. They can either be your own examples, or examples from your everyday reading.

_____

_____

_____

_____

- On the lines below, write a short story about a journey you made, or an adventure that you had, when you were younger:

_____

_____

_____

_____

_____

_____

_____

_____

_____

_____

_____

_____

_____

_____

- Prepare a presentation (4–5 minutes) on a place of interest that you have visited. Consider the points made in 'For a successful presentation:' on p.110. Make notes on the lines below:

_____

_____

_____

_____

_____

_____

_____

_____

_____

_____

_____

_____

_____

_____

_____

_____

_____

_____

_____

Article 11

When Time Began

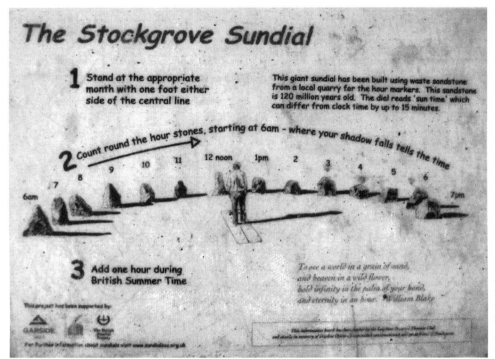

- Look at the two photographs above. They were taken on March 11th, 2012. At approximately what time was the lower photograph taken?

  _____

- It states in the top photograph that 'The sandstone is 120 million years old.' Write 120 million as a number:

  _____

- What, and when, are the equinoxes?

- What is 'Greenwich Mean Time', and when was it established?

- Which famous British scientist wrote 'A Brief History of Time'?

- Sundials are the oldest known devices that are used to measure time. Carry out some research into the history and science of sundials, and write a brief report on the lines below:

- The poem in the bottom right hand corner is not clear, but it reads:

  "To see a world in a grain of sand
  and heaven in a wild flower
  build infinity in the palm of your hand
  and eternity in an hour"

- Who wrote this and what is the name of the poem?

  _____

- In the lines below, reflect on what meaning or feelings the poet is trying to express:

  _____

  _____

  _____

  _____

  _____

- What other well-known poem did this poet write?

  _____

- In the lines below, write a poem on the subject of time and/or any poem of your choice:

  _____

  _____

  _____

  _____

  _____

  _____

  _____

  _____

  _____

  _____

  _____

  _____

Article 12

Distant Thunder
by Satjavit Ray *SUMMARY*

Based on a novel by Bhusan Bannerji, the film is set in 1943-44, when a famine struck Bengal during the British rule in India. It was a man made famine. As the British government cornered the civilian food supply for its armies, the people starved. The famine claimed the lives of five million people.

The story takes place during World War II in a small, tranquil village, where the caste system is strictly observed. The film shows how famine affects the lives of the families in different ways. It is not so much about the famine itself, but the events leading to it at a micro scale. Instead of rotting dead bodies, what we see is the changing life and behaviour of the villagers.

Gangacharan, an educated Brahmin, has recently arrived to settle in the village with his wife. He decides to teach and conduct religious ceremonies in exchange for being supported by the villagers. The villagers readily agree. His wife, Ananga, is a sensuous woman who is thoughtful, giving and devoted to her husband.

The distant World War II changes the village. Gangacharan is only a little more informed than the villagers. He knows that Japan has taken over Singapore but he has no idea where it is. As a few airplanes disturb the peaceful sky, the word goes around that the war will result in a scarcity of rice. The price of rice soars as the traders hide their stocks to make huge profits.

To eat, the villagers are reduced to animal-like existence, forced to beg for food. Gangacharan, shrewd and stingy, has managed to keep himself supplied with food but it may not last long. Ananga offers to work for food but Gangacharan is shocked at the idea of her doing manual labour. Soon, he is forced to change his views and Ananga goes to work with other village women.

A man with burnt face (scarface) offers a married village woman, Chutki, a bribe of rice to go with him. She refuses but later the hunger drives her to agree.

Ananga offers her gold bangle to Gangacharan to exchange it for rice. As he goes to a nearby village to in search of rice, she goes into the forest with Chutki and another woman to look for wild potatoes. The village women find some potatoes. A man tries to take Ananga; Chutki kills the man with the bar she used to dig out the potato.

But Chutki herself would rather live in dishonor than die of hunger. Once again, she joins the scarface despite her revulsion towards him.

As the war-induced rice shortage becomes increasingly acute, the tranquillity of the village is destroyed. Life-long trusts are betrayed. Civil order falls apart. At the same time, the famine prompts some remarkable instances of love and compassion.

An untouchable-caste woman dies of hunger; the first starvation death in the village. Gangacharan, breaking the taboo, picks up her hand take her pulse. He feels obliged to give her a proper cremation.

As the scramble to survive humiliates some of Ray's characters, it ennobles others, including Gangacharan who, towards the end, has begun to question the social system that he has always accepted as given and right. In the context of the film, this is a revolutionary conversion, and a most moving one.

Even as we learn that Ananga is pregnant, we see the villagers leave in search of food in silhouettes. The screen is filled with a statement: "Over five million died of starvation and epidemics in Bengal in what has come to be known as the man-made famine of 1943."

- Describe what the following words mean, and state whether they are nouns, verbs or adjectives:

  Tranquil - _____

  Sensual - _____

  Scarcity - _____

  Shrewd - _____

  Stingy - _____

  Silhouette - _____

  Epidemic - _____

- Explain what is meant by 'the Caste System'

  _____

  _____

  _____

  _____

  _____

- Who was the leader of India's resistance to Britain's colonial rule during the time the film was set, and what his guiding principle?

  _____

  _____

- On the lines below, write a brief review of a film you have seen, or a book you have read, recently. Give an outline of what the film, or book, was about. Consider what it was that you liked, and/or didn't like about the film, or book, and what your favourite, and/or least favourite part, was:

  _____

  _____

  _____

  _____

_____

_____

_____

_____

_____

_____

_____

_____

_____

_____

_____

- Points for class discussion: Which countries, or parts of the world, do you know about where the displacement of people, and/or famine, has occurred.

- Prepare a presentation (4–5 minutes) on a people who have been displaced or who have suffered as a result of famine. Research the events leading up to the displacement or famine. Consider how such events could have been avoided; consider also how such events could be avoided in the future. Consider the points made in 'For a successful presentation:' on p.110. Make notes on the lines below:

_____

_____

_____

_____

_____

_____

_____

_____

_____

_____

_____

_____

Article 13

THE TITANIC

FIRST SAILING OF THE LATEST ADDITION TO THE WHITE STAR FLEET

The Queen of the Ocean

TITANIC

LENGTH 882½ FT.　　　OVER 45,000 TONS　　　BEAM 92½ FT.
TRIPLE-SCREWS

This, the Latest, Largest and Finest Steamer Afloat, will sail from

WHITE STAR LINE, PIER 10, SOUTHAMPTON

WEDNESDAY, APRIL 10TH

en route to NEW YORK

Reservations of Berths may be made direct with this Office or through any of our accredited Agents

THIRD CLASS RATES ARE:

From SOUTHAMPTON, LONDON, LIVERPOOL } £7: 9s : 0d

- Punctuate the following passage

the titanic was built in the shipyards of belfast by fifteen thousand people it took three years to complete and was launched on may 31st 1911 amidst a great fanfare it was a huge liner and was very luxurious the ship could carry three thousand people in her luxurious cabins and was divided into 16 watertight compartments the owners the white star line claimed she was unsinkable

on april 10th 1912 the titanic glided out of southampton harbour bound for new york it was to be her last voyage

on april 14th after four days at sea the ship began to head towards some large packs of ice moving far south from the icy waters of the arctic circle the temperature in the ship began to drop and by 10pm it was at freezing point no-one in charge took the slightest bit of notice

at 11.40pm the ship experienced a staggering crash against a giant iceberg a huge hole was ripped along one third the length of the ship almost straight away the engine rooms began to fill with water

the ships captain edward smith knew the situation was serious and at 12.05am he ordered the lifeboats to be launched saying women and children first as he knew there were not enough on the ship on board that night there were 2,316 passengers a third of these were female before the night was over more than half of the people aboard would be dead

finally at 2am the captain gave his final order every man for himself the remaining passengers and crew looked for safety in the lifeboats but there was only one small lifeboat left 1,503 people were left to go down with the titanic

at about 2.20am the titanic began her final dive into the atlantic people in the sea were sucked under and others were flung off the decks as the ship toppled over finally she slipped beneath the waves

- When was the Titanic's maiden voyage?

  _____

- Who were the owners of the Titanic?

  _____

- Who was the ship's captain?

  _____

- On what date did the Titanic actually sink?

  _____

- What was the length of the ship (to the nearest yard)?

  _____

- What was the width of the ship (to the nearest yard)?

  _____

- How many propellers did the Titanic have?

  _____

- How much would £7: 9s: 0d be in decimal money?

  _____

Article 14

Read the article *Have you joined the Organ Donor Register?* on page **?** and answer the questions that follow it.

- Points for class discussion: Is anyone an organ donor? Do you think that the Organ Donor Register is a good idea? Has anyone thought about becoming an organ donor?

- What is the function of the following organs of the body?

a)   The heart:

_____

_____

b)   The arteries:

_____

_____

c)   The veins:

_____

_____

d)   The stomach:

_____

_____

e)   The small intestine:

_____

_____

f)   The large intestine:

_____

_____

g)   The pancreas:

_____

_____

h)   The liver:

_____

_____

_____

_____

i)   The kidneys:

_____

_____

j)   Sensory neurons:

_____

_____

k)   Motor neurons:

_____

_____

l)   The skeleton:

_____

_____

_____

_____

m) Ligaments and tendons:

_____

_____

n)   The skin:

_____

_____

_____

_____

o)   The hair:

_____

_____

- Prepare a presentation (4–5 minutes) on one of the organs mentioned above. Consider the points made in 'For a successful presentation:' on p.110

Make notes on the lines below, and include a labelled diagram in the space below:

_____

_____

_____

_____

_____

_____

_____

_____

_____

_____

Fact or Opinion?

Look at the following statements, which come from the above 14 articles, and decide if they facts or opinions.

Article 1:

Surbiton, where Liz Green lives, is in Kingston upon Thames. **Fact/Opinion**

The more you have in a class, the harder the teacher's job is. **Fact/Opinion**

Article 2:

Greater emphasis should be placed on Maths and English attainment, particularly in struggling cities. **Fact/Opinion**

Half of all young people in cities without Maths and English GCSE A* to C. **Fact/Opinion**

Article 3:

They lacked a lot of confidence and social skills. It is quite clear the education system has failed them. **Fact/Opinion**

The number of unemployed 16-to-24-year-olds now stands above one million. **Fact/Opinion**

Article 4:

Trevor Huddleston is an inspiration to thousands of people. **Fact/Opinion**

Trevor Huddleston comes from Bedford and was an anti-apartheid campaigner. **Fact/Opinion**

Article 5:

The importance of speaking correctly is becoming ever more relevant in this day and age. **Fact/Opinion**

Elocution can be defined as…

Article 6:

The child-led approach is frequently neither stimulating nor challenging. **Fact/Opinion**

The technique involves children learning the 44 sounds of the English language and how they can be blended together to form words. **Fact/Opinion**

Article 7:

Consumers should begin with one meat-free day a week. **Fact/Opinion**

Rajendra Pachauri, chairman of the UN Intergovernmental Panel on Climate Change, said consumers should begin with one meat-free day a week. **Fact/Opinion**

Article 8:

Camels have nostrils that can close to keep sand at bay. **Fact/Opinion**

Unlike most mammals, a healthy camel's body temperature fluctuates throughout the day from 34°C to 41.7°C (93°F-107°F). **Fact/Opinion**

Article 9:

Kayaking is a really fun sport. **Fact/Opinion**

Play boating is a discipline of white-water kayaking where the paddler performs various technical moves in one place. **Fact/Opinion**

Article 10:

Blantyre is Malawi's second largest city. **Fact/Opinion**

The people of Malawi are really friendly. **Fact/Opinion**

Article 11:

The Stockgrove Sundial was built using local sandstone. **Fact/Opinion**

Sun time can differ from clock time by up to 15 minutes. **Fact/Opinion**

Article 12:

Gangacharan's wife is a sensuous woman. **Fact/Opinion**

Many people starved to death as a result of the famine. **Fact/Opinion**

Article 13:

The owners of the Titanic, the White Star Line, claimed that the Titanic was unsinkable. **Fact/Opinion**

"The Titanic is unsinkable!" **Fact/Opinion**

Article 14:

You can join the NHS Organ Donor Register by calling 0300 123 23 23 **Fact/ Opinion**

People in their 70s and 80s have become organ donors. **Fact/Opinion**

Quick Quiz

Which day is celebrated in Britain on March 1st?

_____

How is that day celebrated?

_____

What famous discovery was made on March 1st 1896 and by whom?

_____

Which famous British architect was born on March 1st, 1812?

_____

Name a famous building that he designed?

_____

Which famous British writer was born in the same year?

_____

Name 6 books that he wrote.

_____

_____

_____

Which famous British scientist was born in February, 1809?

_____

Which book did he write?

_____

Which day is celebrated on March 8th?

_____

Which famous Florentine early Renaissance painter was born on March 1st?

_____

Which 'teen idol' was born on March 1st 1994?

_____

Speaking and Listening

Holding a discussion – Good Practice:

- Plan and prepare what you are going to say.
- Make relevant contributions, but do not dominate the discussion.
- Respond appropriately to others.
- Listen actively to others and try not to interrupt.
- Speak clearly and use appropriate language.
- Stick to the subject matter.
- Ask questions – 'What do you think … ?'

For a successful presentation:

- Research your subject thoroughly and make notes etc
- Plan and prepare how you are going to deliver your presentation e.g. power-point slides, use of realia etc.
- Familiarise yourself with your presentation through practising, and timing, it.
- Introduce your topic.
- Present information and ideas clearly and persuasively.
- Face and engage all members of the audience through eye contact.
- Give your own point of view.
- Make conclusions/recommendations.
- Sum up at the end.
- Ask for, and anticipate, any questions

The justification for focussing on the importance of developing speaking and listening skills in adult learners is highlighted in the Adult Literacy Core Curriculum (2001: 20) which states that, 'Speaking and listening is by far the most widespread form of communication even in the most literate person's life', and that the majority of people at work 'spend much more time speaking, listening and discussing than reading or writing'. However, despite the fact that difficulties with speaking and listening can have a major effect on the ways adults function in everyday life and in society as a whole, they are often the least considered or identified literacy skill.

It is useful to separate the idea of listening to what people say from the noise that people make when they talk. 'Hearing' a person means picking up the sounds they make. 'Listening' on the other hand is a skill which involves hearing another person's words, remembering them, thinking about what they mean and planning what to say back to that person. In order to remember what someone has said, it has to be understood first. There are degrees of listening ranging from poor or 'brick wall' listening, to good or 'active/empathetic' listening.

'Brick wall' listening involves lack of eye contact, giving no verbal response and showing disinterest by poor body posture or turning away.

'Active' or 'empathetic' listening involves making eye contact, acknowledging what has been said and giving verbal responses, nodding and body posture.

Developing listening skills involves developing **accuracy** and **efficiency**. Listening **accurately** means:

- Remembering specific relevant information.

- Knowing what to expect to hear.

- Recognising elements of natural, connected speech.

Listening **efficiently** means:

- Being able to follow the structure of talk (i.e. 'keep track')

- Being able to distinguish between important and unimportant information (i.e. to 'get the gist')

- Making use of context to guess, predict and interpret meaning.

Possible barriers to listening can include:

- Lack of empathy, or poor relationship, between speaker and listener.

- Talking too quickly with few pauses.

- Unfamiliar vocabulary and phrases/metaphors/colloquialisms.

- Unfamiliar subject or lack of interest in subject.

- Cultural barriers.

- Unfamiliar accent.

- Lack of concentration over long periods of time.

- Interruptions when there are many people talking together.

Possible barriers to good speaking can include:

- Lack of confidence.

- Lack of knowledge/suitable vocabulary.

- Cultural restraints.

- Lack of appropriateness (being aware of appropriate language for a particular situation/context).

What are the factors affecting individual speech?

Volume of voice (quiet or loud); pitch of voice (low or high); tone of voice (monotonous or varied); regional dialect; regional accent; lexical choice; situational factors; personality; social influences; educational influences.

Strategies for developing speaking and listening skills could include:

- Use of a range of role play scenarios (e.g. mock interview – interviewer/ interviewee; speaking in court; doctor/patient etc.) followed by discussion relating to the appropriateness of the language used.

- Listening to a presentation, and answering questions relating to the 'gist' and overall understanding on the one hand, and specific detail/key relevant points on the other.

- Listening to dvd and telephone recordings, and in pairs, compare how a listener provides feedback and confirmation face to face, and on the telephone.

- Sitting back to back in pairs. One learner describes a diagram, whilst the other draws it from the description. Discuss importance and use of body language.

- Exercises to test and increase range of vocabulary, followed by preparing and delivering a short presentation on a given subject to include use of new vocabulary (For examples here, refer to discussion-based articles).

- Listening to, and transcribing, a short conversation between two speakers whereby one is using Standard English, and the other non-standard English, followed by a comparison of the dialects in terms of the grammar and vocabulary used, and accents in terms of the pronunciation used.

- Group discussion on why listening is important, to include the 'DOs' and 'DONTs' of listening and what makes a 'good listener.'

- Group discussion on importance of clarity, tone, pitch and volume of voice in a variety of everyday situations (e.g. talking to a friend, a colleague, the boss, a child, an old person etc; addressing a group of teenagers, parents, colleagues, interviewers etc.)

- Group discussion on whether or not there are situations where it is appropriate to challenge, or correct, the grammar and pronunciation used in non-standard English and if so, when.

- Focus during discussions on importance of turn taking, not dominating the discussion and bringing in others.

Writing letters

In terms of writing skills in general, I frequently hear it being said that an increasing number of young people are actually losing the ability to write. Text messaging is frequently held out as a factor, but I think there's a lot more to it than that, since apparently it was people with quite a high level of literacy skills who developed simplified ways of text messaging. More importantly, I believe, are issues discussed earlier, such as low levels of expectations on teachers' and students' writing skills and the lack of constant and consistent error correction in both written and spoken English throughout many students' education.

When discussing letter writing, two types are introduced, namely informal and formal. Following discussion and examples of what each are, I ask which of the two is more common. The answer given is invariably 'formal letters' and further discussion reveals the fact that informal letters to friends are rarely written these days, with the blame going to the increased use of email, text messaging and social networking sites etc. particularly amongst the younger generation, and the range of electronic devices that support them, as a replacement for the nearly defunct personal letter. I do at this juncture however, let the class know that my Aunty Doris (from Washington) and my Aunty Jean (in Workington) have been writing to each other once a week for the past 60 years!

The aforementioned Writing Works provides a variety of examples of formal letters, and encourages the development of formal letter writing skills through its writing frames, which provide step by step guidance for learners to follow. In addition, the bbcskllswise website provides a range of letter writing exercises, including proofreading letters for spelling, punctuation and grammatical errors.

The following examples show a range of formal letters including a letter of complaint, a letter of support, a letter of application, and a letter of enquiry.

In each case, learners can be reminded of the layout of the letter, including position of the writer's and recipient's address, date, salutation and correct spelling and usage of 'Yours faithfully' and 'Yours sincerely'(related to whether or not the writer knows the name of the person they are writing to), and the position of the writer's printed name beneath the signature.

In each letter also, there are a range of common spelling, punctuation and grammatical errors, feedback on which can be used as opportunities to reinforce any relevant rules and links to word classes, for example with the spelling of practice and effect (as nouns), and practise and affect (as verbs) etc.

Formal letter of complaint

26 Burley Rd
Hayford
West Yorkshire
HY2 4ET

February 17th 2012

The Manager
Morsco Supemarket
Market Square
Hayford HY3 2SD

Dear Sir or Madam

I am writing to complain about the standard of servise that I received in your supermarket yesterday evening. I decided to try out the new self-service checkouts, which you have recently had installed, in order to check out there affectiveness. Unfortunatly however, the machine didn't seem to be working propely and an annoying automated voice kept saying, "please remove unwanted items in the bagging area!" Each time this happened, I had to call for assistance and wait for what seemed like ages for someone to come and sort the problem out. Who knows, maybe I need more practise?

   I wouldn't of minded having to wait for so long if the supermarket had actualy been busy, but each time the store assistance arrived to sort out the problem, he became more and more abrupt. Furthermore, he failed to apologise for keeping me waiting. I hope that by the time I visit your store next, that you will have either had the oppurtunity to improve the self-service checkouts or the customer service standards of your shop asistants!

Yours faithfuly

Kevin Norley

Formal letter of enquiry

18 Caversham Street
Fersham Green
Rutland
FS2 8JR

February 17th, 2012

Mr Dean
Mercury Leisure Centre
Fersham Green
Rutland FS1 0QT

Dear Mr Dean

A coleague of mine has recently informed me that there may be new Zumba and Capoiera classes starting at the Mercury liesure Centre in the new year. I would apreciate it if you could provide me with details of the classes i.e. the time and date and cost etc. In addition, I would be greateful if you could send me details of other fitness classes that you run, and any broshures or leaflets you may have concerning the cost of Leisure Centre, and gym, membership etc.

   From what I can understand, there will be less childrens' swimming classes at the leisure centre next year, due to the local contractors on-going maintainence work occurring at the centre. If that is so, could you please let me know which classes will still be running, and when the full schedual of swimming classes are likely to return to normal.
I look forward to hearing from you.

Yours sinserely

Kevin Norley

Formal letter of thanks

84 Crossfield Rd
Tottenham
London
N14 4UR

February 10th, 2012

The manager
Hotpot Restaurant
Orange Bear St (off Leicester Square)
London
WC1

Dear Madam

On Wednesday evening, my friends and I enjoyed a really good performance of the new Billy Elliot musical at a theatre in the West End. Before the play started, we decided to go for a meal in the Leicester Square area. We didn't have a lot of time, so I reccomended to them that we should go to the Hotpot. We didn't have a lot of money either, not after 'forking out so much for our theatre tickets anyway. Even though your restaurant was clearly very busy, you found us a table quite quickly after just a short wait. The service was then exellent; your waitresses and waiter's was polite, efficient and friendly. The food was very good and, considering its the West End, very reasonably priced.

   My friends have told me that when they go to the theatre again, either with other people, or again with me, they will try more dishes from your traditional menu of Anglo European cuisine. I would also like to add that I have been coming to your restaurant, and it's sister restaurant, The West End Diner, for several years now and have always, without exeption, enjoyed really good service and really good food!
Thank you again.

Yours faithfully

Kevin Norley

Formal letter of application

26 The Link
Cardiff
South Glamorgan
CF1 2EP

February 10th, 2012

Mrs J Griffiths
Human Resources Manager
Renewable Energy Centre
Silverlink Way
Cardiff
South Glamorgan
CF6 7JP

Dear Mrs Griffiths

Further to your recent job advertisment in the Cardiff Chronicle, dated 7th June 2011, I am applying for the position of trainee energy apprentise.

As you can see from my CV, I have recent voluntery work experience. This provided me with the opportunity to become familier with dealing with customer's on a daily basis, and aloud me to become accustomed to having a daily work routine.As you can also see from my CV, I have recently acheived a level 2 qualification in adult literacy and a level 1 qualification in adult numeracy, and am currently working towards my level 2 at Barnford college.

I have good communication skills and am IT literate. I am reliable, keen and willing to learn new skills, and to undergo any training that is necesary for the job roll. I have read about your company and the training that your aprenticeship programme offers, and believe that my skills and experience, combined with a high level of motivation, make me a suitible candidate for the position.

I enclose a CV for your perusal and look forward to hearing from you in due course.

Yours sincerely

Kevin Norley

Formal letter of apology

17 Oxford Rd
Newminster
Suffolk
NM3 4TY

February 10th, 2012

Mr Haleem
Urnsford College of Further Education
Newminster
Suffolk
NM2 1JP

Dear Mr haleem

I wish to inform you that unfortunatley I shall no longer be able to attend the Complimentary Therapies course at the College. This is dew to the fact that my work comittments have increased over the past few weeks which, combined with my family obligations, means that I will no longer be able to attend all my sessions and complete the necessary coursework.

I would like to apologise for any inconvenients that my withdrawal may cause and to take this opportunity to let you know that I have enjoyed your classes, particulaly the anatomy and phisiology ones, and to thank you for having taught me over the past term. I have learnt a lot about the different types of complimentary therapy treatments and experienced directly many of their theraputic effects.

I would also like to let you know that if my situation changes over the next few months, that I shall consider re-enroling in september, during the next academic year.

Yours sincerely

Kevin Norley

• On the lines below, practise writing a formal letter of complaint, thanks, enquiry, application and apology:

The following three letters have been written to a local MP (name has been altered) do not leave much doubt as to where I stand on certain issues relating to literacy and numeracy in its wider context, as discussed in the previous part of this book.

Letter 1

26 Arcadian Road
Ferryside
Dyfed
SA17 4UT

May 30th 2012

The Chief Executive
Institute for Learning
First Floor
49 – 51 East Road
Old Street
London
N1 6AH

Dear Madam

I am writing to you with regard to issues I have concerning the poor numeracy standards of many people in this country and its possible causes, including the lack of professionalization within the further education and skills sector.

In a recent *review of research and evaluation on improving adult literacy and numeracy skills,* published by the Department for Business, Innovation and Skills, it was found that learner progress in numeracy is greater where teachers are qualified in maths to Level 3 or above.

In my book Making Britain Numerate (2nd Ed), published in October, 2011, I stated that, ' … during my experience in the post-16 sector (including FE colleges and private training providers), I have observed that many of the tutors delivering functional skills (previously key skills) maths, or adult numeracy, do not have a level 3 maths qualification.' and that 'It is generally understood, and expected, in teaching that those who are delivering a particular subject should themselves be well qualified in that subject, and at the very least, be one level above the students they are teaching.' It does not appear to be the case then, when it comes to the teaching of functional skills maths or adult numeracy.

Furthermore, in terms of the entry requirements onto post-compulsory Certificate of Education (Cert Ed) courses, I have noticed that students have been able to enter onto the course and achieve their Cert Ed qualification without obtaining a level 2 numeracy qualification. The only requirement then seems to be that they must achieve a level 2 numeracy qualification if, and when, they try and obtain QTLS status (Qualified Teacher in the Lifelong Learning Sector). Even then, this can be obtained by simply achieving a level 2 pass in adult numeracy with 19 out of 40 in a level 2 adult numeracy multiple choice test.

To deal with the competition in the job market within the context of today's economic climate, I have heard reports of employers preferring applicants to have 4 good GCSEs (i.e. grades A – C), including maths and English, before offering places on apprenticeship programmes. It seems rather odd to me then, that it is possible to obtain a Cert Ed teaching qualification without achieving a bare minimum level 2 adult numeracy qualification (i.e. a level 2 GCSE 'equivalent' qualification), yet in order to be considered for some apprenticeship programmes, GCSEs in both maths and English are becoming necessary!

I have argued on many occasions, over a period of years, that a level 2 maths qualification should be part of a stringent admissions policy for teachers entering the post-16 sector, and that that qualification should either be a GCSE in maths (grade A – C) or a level 2 functional maths qualification (but not a far less rigorous level 2 adult numeracy qualification).

I believe that the low level of expectations of teachers' numeracy skills correlates directly with a low level of expectations of students' skills and with the current low level of student achievement in functional skills maths. I also believe that there is a correlation between young people's low numeracy and literacy skills and, in the context of reports from employers claiming that young British people don't have the required skills in order to obtain work (along with a widely held perception that this is the case), the current high rate of youth unemployment.

As the IfL is the professional body for teachers, tutors, trainers and student teachers in the further education (FE) and skills sector, I would appreciate it if you would address the above issues and concerns that I have raised. In addition, I would appreciate it if you would highlight these issues and concerns with John Hayes, the Further Education and Skills Minister, and seek from him both explanations and solutions for them. I would also appreciate it if you would pass on my recommendations to him so that he can inform the review panel that he has convened, which is looking at the 'current arrangements to regulate and facilitate the professionalism of the FE and Skills workforce.'

I look forward to hearing from you.

Yours sincerely

Kevin Norley FIFL, QTLS

Letter 2

26 Arcadian Road
Ferryside
Dyfed
SA17 4UT

May 30th 2012

Member of Parliament
House of Common
London
WC1A OAA

Dear Member of Parliament

I am writing to you with my concerns over the rising youth unemployment level in this country, which currently stands at just above one million people (16 – 24 year olds). As you will be aware, many reports have appeared in the press over recent years stating that employers (for example large supermarket chains) in this country believe that many young British people either do not have the work ethic or suitable skills (including English and maths skills) to gain employment. There have also been reports decrying poor English standards.

I have worked in education for over twenty years and have seen at first hand, literally on a daily basis, a direct correlation between students' spoken English and communication skills, and their reading and writing skills, and hence their level of qualifications. In turn then, there is a direct correlation between people's qualifications and their chances of obtaining employment and/or higher education. Related to this, I have also noticed over the years that the majority of unemployed people do not speak using Standard English. There is a lot of evidence indicating that the ability to read and write 'feeds' directly off speaking and listening. There is also a lot of evidence to suggest that the failure of a large proportion of working class children in education is due to the 'dialectic mismatch' that exists between students in our schools and their teachers, who do, predominantly, use Standard English.

I believe strongly therefore that there is a compelling case for elocution, and/or the constant and consistent correction of grammar, to be introduced to all state schools (primary and secondary) across the country. Elocution would reduce this dialectic mismatch, hence giving students greater access to all parts of the curriculum.

This would, I believe, serve as a way to counteract the injustices that have been inflicted on the financially and culturally less well-off people in our society, and be part of the solution towards ensuring our young people are able to become more actively engaged in their education and hence more qualified with a better chance of finding employment.

I would appreciate it if you would highlight the issues I have raised, and the potential solution to them, with the Education Secretary and seek a response from him.

I look forward to hearing from you.

Yours sincerely

Kevin Norley

Letter 3

26 Arcadian Road
Ferryside
Dyfed
SA17 4UT

May 30ᵗʰ 2012

Member of Parliament
House of Common
London
WC1A OAA

Dear Member of Parliament

Please could you confirm and give assurances that since the coalition parties have been in Government in this country, no 'arms' or surveillance technology have been sent by any British company to any dictatorships for use against their own people, or people of neighbouring countries.

I believe that the clear view of the majority of British people would be that to send any form of weapons to countries which could use them to oppress any people would be morally wrong.

This letter reflects my desire and, I believe, the desire of many, to live in a civilised society. I look forward to hearing from you.

Yours sincerely

Kevin Norley

Functional Skills
Reading and Writing– 1

Document 1 – Reading for Research

Childhood Obesity

In the past year, children's diets and eating habits have rarely been out of the headlines. Dietician Juliette Kellow looks at the size of the child obesity problem and gives parents some top tips for keeping their children healthy and in great shape.

The Shocking Facts

Childhood obesity is big news and unfortunately, like the waistbands of our nation's children and teenagers, it's set to get even bigger.

Childhood Obesity Statistics

Statistics from the most recent large-scale survey in the UK shockingly reveal that 25 percent of boys and 33 percent of girls aged between two and 19 years are overweight or obese – and there's little sign the incidence is slowing.

Obesity currently costs the country around £2 billion annually and shortens lives by nine years, due to the associated health problems. Some health experts even believe we'll soon see parents outliving their children.

Equally worrying is the fact that parents are getting so used to seeing overweight kids, they don't recognise their own children are obese.

Last year, a study from the Peninsula Medical School in Plymouth, revealed that:

- three quarters of parents failed to recognise their child was overweight.

- 33 percent of mums and 57 percent of dads considered their child's weight to be 'about right' when, in fact, they were obese.

- one in ten parents expressed some concern about their child being underweight when they were actually a normal, healthy weight.

Risks of Obesity in Children

Health experts are particularly worried about this in view of the health risks linked with obesity, which include heart disease, certain cancers, high blood pressure, joint problems, psychological difficulties and diabetes.

An American study in the 90s showed that overweight teenagers were eight and a half times more likely to develop high blood pressure and almost 2 and a half times as likely to have high blood cholesterol levels.

Meanwhile, in recent years there's been an alarming rise in the number of children being diagnosed with Type 2 diabetes, a condition that's typically seen in overweight middle-aged adults. Diabetes UK believes there are currently around 100 children with the condition, although some experts believe the figure could be as high as 1,400 based on the number of overweight and obese schoolchildren there are in the UK. Experts relate this solely to the increase in childhood obesity.

Why are our Children Getting so Fat?

Unfortunately, there's no mystery! Quite simply, many children do little exercise and eat a diet that's packed with junk food.

School Dinners and Junk Food

Numerous studies confirm what celebrity chef Jamie Oliver discovered when he started looking more closely at school dinners – that children consume too much sugar, salt and saturates and eat only two portions of fruit and veg each day.

The problems start early in life. A survey by Mother & Baby magazine in 2004 revealed that nine out of 10 toddlers eat junk food, with chocolate, biscuits, crisps, fish fingers, chips, cake and chicken nuggets appearing in their top 10 favourite foods.

And this is just the tip of the iceberg – children's diets generally get worse as they get older and more food is eaten outside the home. Indeed, according to school dinners catering company Sodexho, eight to 16 year olds spend £549 million a year on the way to and from school, mostly on confectionery, crisps and fizzy drinks – an increase of 213 percent in just seven years!

How Can We Stop our Children from Piling on the Pounds?

Unsurprisingly, most health experts agree one of the most important factors in the fight against childhood obesity is to encourage healthy eating habits from an early age.

Document 2

Cigarettes, diet, alcohol and obesity behind more than 100,000 cancers

Wednesday 7 December 2011 · Cancer Research UK Press Release

More than 100,000 cancers – equivalent to one third of all those diagnosed in the UK each year – are being caused by smoking, unhealthy diets, alcohol and excess weight, according to new research* by Cancer Research UK.

This figure further increases to around 134,000 when taking into account all 14 lifestyle and environmental risk factors** analysed in this study.

This new review of cancer and lifestyle in the UK is the most comprehensive undertaken to date and is published today (Wednesday) in a supplement to the British Journal of Cancer.

Smoking is far and away the most important lifestyle factor causing 23 per cent of cancers in men and 15.6 per cent in women (nearly one in five cancers).

Overall the review shows that 45 per cent of all cancers in men could be prevented – compared with 40 per cent of all cancers in women.

Professor Max Parkin, a Cancer Research UK epidemiologist based at Queen Mary, University of London, and study author, said "Many people believe cancer is down to fate or 'in the genes' and that it is the luck of the draw whether they get it.

"Looking at all the evidence, it's clear that around 40 per cent of all cancers are caused by things we mostly have the power to change.

"We didn't expect to find that eating fruit and vegetables would prove to be so important in protecting men against cancer. And among women we didn't expect being overweight to have a greater effect than alcohol.

"In most cases cancers have multiple causes – for example a cervical cancer can be linked to both HPV infection and smoking. This means it isn't possible to add up the effects of different lifestyle factors – you'd get more than 100 per cent."***

In this study, the top six risk factors were calculated as follows (the number of cases has been rounded to the nearest hundred).

Of the 158,700 cancers diagnosed in men each year:

Risk Factor	Cancers linked to each risk factor	
	Percentage	Number
Tobacco	23	36,500
Lack of fruit and vegetables	6.1	9,600
Occupation (eg exposure to asbestos)	4.9	7,800
Alcohol	4.6	7,300
Overweight and obesity	4.1	6,500
Excessive sun exposure and sunbeds	3.5	5,500

Of the 155,600 cancers diagnosed in women each year:

Risk Factor	Cancers linked to each risk factor	
	Percentage	Number
Tobacco	15.6	24,300
Overweight and obesity	6.9	10,800
Infections (e.g. HPV)	3.7	5,800
Excessive sun exposure and sunbeds	3.6	5,600
Lack of fruit and vegetables	3.4	5,300
Alcohol	3.3	5,100

Overall total including all 14 risk factors	Percentage of cancers linked to a combination of 14 factors	Number of cancers linked to a combination of 14 factors
Men	45.3	72,000
Women	40.1	62,000
Men and Women	42.7	134,000

Please note: some cancers are caused by more than one factor, so adding these columns won't result in the total number of cancers caused by lifestyle.

CANCER RESEARCH UK

More than
100,000 cancers
diagnosed in the UK each year are being caused by **smoking**, unhealthy **diets, alcohol** and excess **weight**

60,000 caused by smoking
100,000 caused by all of the above

Together we will beat cancer

Overall, one in 25 cancers is linked to occupation and one in 33 to infections.

It is estimated that tobacco smoking, dietary factors, drinking alcohol and bodyweight account for 106,845 or 34 per cent of cancers occurring in 2010. This is based on predicted numbers of cancer cases in 2010, using UK incidence figures for the 15-year period from 1993 to 2007.

Sara Hiom, director of information at Cancer Research UK, said: "We know, especially during the Christmas party season, that it is hard to watch what you eat and limit alcohol and we don't want people to feel guilty about having a drink or indulging a bit more than usual. However, it's very important for people to understand that long term changes to their lifestyles can really reduce their cancer risk."

Dr Harpal Kumar, Cancer Research UK's chief executive, said: "Leading a healthy life doesn't guarantee that a person won't get cancer but this study shows that healthy habits can significantly stack the odds in our favour.

"While we have made tremendous progress in improving the chance of surviving cancer during the last 40 years, we need to make sure people are made aware of the risks of getting the disease in the first place so they can make the healthiest possible lifestyle choices.

"We know that cancer risk can be affected by family history and getting older, but these figures show that we can take positive steps to help reduce our risk of the disease. Stopping smoking, eating a balanced diet, cutting down on alcohol and maintaining a healthy weight could be New Year's resolutions that help save more lives in future."

Activity 1 - Reading for research

Having read documents 1 and 2, answer the following questions:

1. What do the two documents have in common?

   _____

   _____

2. According to document 1, what are the main two reasons why a greater proportion of children are becoming obese?

   _____

   _____

3. According to document 1, state two reasons why childhood obesity is a cause for concern.

   _____

   _____

4. In document 1, under the heading 'Childhood Obesity Statistics', identify from the first paragraph:

   Two nouns: _____

   Two verbs: _____

   Two adjectives: _____

   One adverb: _____

5. According to document 1, what does celebrity chef Jamie Oliver think that school dinners contain too much of?

   _____

   _____

6. According to document 2, which risk factors for cancer are amongst the six most common risk factors for men and women?

   _____

   _____

7. Look at document 2. Name 2 factors that can influence cancer risk, but that are not affected by lifestyle.

_____

_____

8. According to document 2, what four things can a person do, in relation to their lifestyle, in order to reduce the risk of getting cancer?

_____

_____

9. According to document 2, where was the new research by Cancer Research UK published?

_____

_____

10. According to document 2 how many cases of cancer in women each year are linked to being overweight?

_____

_____

Activity 2 - Writing a report

You are a member of the Parent Teacher Association Committee of your local school. Children's diet is on the agenda for the next meeting.

Using documents 1 and 2, produce a report for the committee highlighting what you believe to be the main issues concerning the diets of school children. Make recommendations in your report to address the issue of rising obesity levels of young people in today's society, and what the potential consequences might be if no action were to be taken.

In your report, you should:

- Summarise in your own words the main points and ideas from the documents

- Focus on writing clearly, accurate punctuation, grammar and spelling, and writing in paragraphs.

_____

_____

_____

_____

Activity 3 - Writing a letter

During the meeting, it is suggested that you write a letter to be sent to parents and guardians, the aim of which is to encourage parents to ensure their children have a healthy diet, and to inform them of the potential problems to children caused by obesity.

In your letter you should:

- Try and give advice and make suggestions, but without being patronising.

- Focus on writing clearly, accurate punctuation, grammar and spelling, and writing in paragraphs.

_____

_____

_____

_____

_____

_____

_____

_____

_____

_____

_____

_____

_____

_____

_____

_____

_____

_____

Activity 4

In January 2012, the Department for Health (DH: Public health, adult social care and the NHS) launched its nationwide campaign, entitled 'Change4Life', to help us plan affordable, healthier meals. Using the internet, carry out some research into this and some further research into obesity in general, and childhood obesity in particular. Make some notes on the lines below:

_____

_____

_____

_____

_____

_____

_____

_____

_____

_____

_____

_____

_____

_____

_____

_____

_____

_____

_____

_____

_____

_____

_____

Functional Skills
Reading and Writing - 2

Document 1

Solar Power vs. Wind Energy – You decide!

WIND POWER is the conversion of wind energy into a useful form of energy, such as using wind turbines to make electricity, windmills for mechanical power, wind pumps for water pumping or drainage, or sails to propel ships.

Areas where winds are stronger and more constant, such as offshore and high altitude sites, are preferred locations for wind farms. Typical capacity factors are 20-40%, with values at the upper end of the range in particularly favourable sites.

Globally, the long-term technical potential of wind energy is believed to be five times total current global energy production, or 40 times current electricity demand. This could require wind turbines to be installed over large areas, particularly in areas of higher wind resources. Offshore resources experience mean wind speeds of ~90% greater than that of land, so offshore resources could contribute substantially more energy.

A large wind farm may consist of several hundred individual wind turbines which are connected to the electric power transmission network. Offshore wind power can harness the better wind speeds that are available offshore compared to on land, so offshore wind power's contribution in terms of electricity supplied is higher. Small onshore wind facilities are used to provide electricity to isolated locations and utility companies increasingly buy back surplus electricity produced by small domestic wind turbines. Although a variable source of power, the intermittency of wind seldom creates problems when using wind power to supply up to 20% of total electricity demand, but as the proportion rises, increased costs, a need to use storage such as pumped-storage hydroelectricity, upgrade the grid, or a lowered ability to supplant conventional production may occur. Power management techniques such as excess capacity, storage, dispatchable backing supply (usually natural gas), exporting and importing power to neighboring areas or reducing demand when wind production is low, can mitigate these problems.

Wind power, as an alternative to fossil fuels, is plentiful, renewable, widely distributed, clean, produces no greenhouse gas emissions during operation, and uses little land. In operation, the overall cost per unit of energy produced is similar to the cost for new coal and natural gas installations. The construction of wind farms is not universally welcomed, but any effects on the environment from wind power are generally much less problematic than those of any other power source.

The most frequently cited objections to wind turbines seem to be noise and the potential impacts on birds, but other issues have included aesthetics (their perceived intrusiveness on the landscape) as well as "shadow flicker" which is the flickering effect caused when rotating wind turbine blades periodically cast shadows through constrained openings such as the windows of neighbouring properties.

However, the main issue that restricts the use of wind energy (using existing methods of harvesting) are its relatively low efficiency and more importantly, the unreliable nature of the resource. Unlike tide energy (which can be predicted accurately) wind energy is extremely intermittent as there is considerable variability in wind speed, intensity, duration and even wind direction. As a result, batteries are generally needed for wind power because it doesn't provide constant power.

The intermittency of the wind is what rules out many locations from having wind turbines, and even where the (measured) wind patterns demonstrate its feasibility, there will always be "down time" when the wind is insufficient and these are difficult, if not impossible, to accurately predict.

As a result of its intermittent, poorly predictable nature, wind can make a useful contribution as a supplementary electricity source, but using the current turbine designs, it remains unlikely that it could ever be dominant. These problems of intermittency are less likely for wind farms in offshore locations, since the lower friction associated with the sea surface (in comparison to wind blowing over the land surface) results in less problems with source variability; however, the installation and maintenance costs are higher for the offshore windfarms, and they are likely to be located further away from existing electricity grids.

Notwithstanding these factors, there is ongoing research into alleviating some of the problems of wind power including noise and voltage dips.

....

SOLAR ENERGY is the energy derived from the sun through the form of solar radiation. Solar powered electrical generation relies on photovoltaics and heat engines. A partial list of other solar applications includes space heating and cooling through solar architecture, daylighting, solar hot water, solar cooking, and high temperature process heat for industrial purposes.

Solar technologies are broadly characterized as either passive solar or active solar depending on the way they capture, convert and distribute solar energy. Active solar techniques include the use of photovoltaic panels and solar thermal collectors to harness the energy. Passive solar techniques include orienting a building to the Sun, selecting materials with favorable thermal mass or light dispersing properties, and designing spaces that naturally circulate air.

Monocrystalline solar cell.

So, it is inevitable that the production and use of solar technology will have an environmental impact. However, that is also true of all other systems used for energy generation, distribution and consumption (whether from renewable or non-renewable sources). The most important issue is a comparison, for each available energy option, of how the technology's performance balances against its various environmental "footprints".

As such, even though there are potential impacts to the environment from using solar energy sources, the most important issue is how this compares to other sources of energy, and how the identified impacts can be reduced, controlled and mitigated.

Even though the production of the technology may affect the environment, and they have limitations for their use (day-time only; sufficient solar intensity, etc.) requiring the use of storage batteries, the main advantage is the lack of pollution or GHG emissions associated with their actual operation.

Another positive of solar is the devices that the actual maintenance should also be simpler. A wind energy conversion system is structurally more complex and is mechanically-based, as compared to, for example, a photovoltaic system which is based on electronics and electrical systems (solar radiation converted to electricity by semi-conductors). Devices using solar energy for direct heating (e.g. water heaters, crop dryers) would have even less maintenance issues.

Solar panels are less intrusive than big wind turbines. Solar devices are almost maintenance free once set up and are equally scalable (i.e. it is easy to add panels to an existing system.

In general you would have solar power for small amounts of power (like a small number of electronic devices). Even more so, if the location is remote like weather monitoring stations or satellites.

Wind would be the better option if you want to produce a significant amount of power. Wind farms would be better than solar farms if replacing power plants.

If you want to power a home, I believe that wind is probably still the most cost-effective method unless you consume a very small amount of power.

Document 2

ENERGYCARE GROUP SOLAR ELECTRICITY PROGRAMME 2011

OPTION 1:

100% FREE SOLAR ELECTRICITY

Thanks to a new Government backed scheme, EnergyCare Group is able to supply and install solar photovoltaic (PV) systems 100% FREE OF CHARGE. This offer is available to all homeowners, landlords, schools, Housing Association and commercial properties that have a south-facing roof.

Benefits

With soaring fuel prices the property owner will benefit from free electricity the solar system generates and will save up to 50% of their annual bill with no outlay whatsoever (savings dependant on size of system). Please call for further details.

....

OPTION 2:

PURCHASE YOUR OWN SOLAR ELECTRICITY SYSTEM

The customer invests in a solar photovoltaic system through EnergyCare Group (typical cost of average system including installation is between £6,000 to £12,000 dependant on roof size), and in return the customer will receive the full Feed-In Tariff over the 25 year term. This Feed-In Tariff (FITS) is a 25 year Government index linked pay back scheme and works as follows.

- Your electricity supplier will pay you 43.3p per unit (Kwh) generated.
- You will also get paid 3.1p for every unit you export back to the National Grid.
- Depending on the size of your roof and location, you could generate an annual income of over £1,000.
- With electricity prices set to soar and the pay back index linked for 25 years the money you make/save will increase
- This could equate to a profit of over £35,000 over the 25 year contract period
- The money you make is TAX FREE!

APPROVED INSTALLER

RENEWABLE ENERGY ASSURANCE LIMITED

HOW DO YOU APPLY?
Simply contact EnergyCare Group on ▮▮▮▮ ▮▮▮ ▮▮▮▮ to arrange a FREE survey

Reprinted with kind permission of EnergyCare Group, Haynes, Bedfordshire UK

Document 3

Are you interested in learning new skills?

Increase your employment prospects in the low carbon future **free** of charge

Colleges across East of England are offering unemployed individuals the chance to learn new skills or to improve their current skills. Training sessions last from 1 to 3 days and equip participants with recognised knowledge, skills and qualifications currently in demand.

Training options include basic knowledge as well as in depth courses including

- Introduction to renewable energy
- Sustainable procurement
- Awareness of energy efficiency and its implementation
- Rainwater harvesting
- Sustainable development practises
- Electrical installation
- Hot water heating systems

The Government has set challenging targets for increasing the use of renewable energy, water conservation and reducing fuel poverty. By providing additional training opportunities we intend to help meet those targets.

For further information and to find out more about training opportunities please contact SSDAdmistrator@bedford.ac.uk

Reprinted with kind permission of Bedford College

Activity 1 – Reading for Research

Having read documents 1, 2 and 3, answer the following questions:

1. Look at document 1. Name 3 advantages and 3 disadvantages of both solar and wind power.

   _____

   _____

   _____

   _____

   _____

   _____

2. Look at document 1. Identify a disadvantage that both forms of energy have in common.

   _____

   _____

3. Look at document 1. Which would be more cost-effective to power the following:

   a) A remote house in the remote highlands of Scotland?

   _____

   b) A weather monitoring station?

   _____

   c) A school in an urban area?

   _____

   d) The replacement for a power plant?

   _____

4. What is the main purpose of document 1?

   a) To advertise
   b) To inform
   c) To compare
   d) To criticise

5. The arguments for and against the use of solar energy and wind power in document 1 can best be described as:

   a) One-sided
   b) Balanced

c) Exaggerated

d) Biased

6. Look at document 1. How does the overall cost per unit of energy of wind farms compare with the overall cost per unit of energy for natural gas installations?

7. Match the following words from the document 1(column A) with a word that is similar in meaning (column B):

Column A	Column B
supplant	ability
procured	unavoidable
potential (adj)	sporadic
cited	orthodox
harness	replace
conventional	corrosive
intermittent	utilise
inevitable	reported in
potential (n)	obtained
caustic	possible

8. What is the main purpose of document 2?

a) To persuade

b) To inform

c) To instruct

d) To compare

9. Look at document 2. In which of the two options is there an initial charge for the solar photovoltaic system to be fitted?

10. Look at document 2. In option 2, what will a person's income from the installation of the solar photovoltaic system depend on?

11. Look at document 2. What techniques does the writer use in order to enhance his or her message?

12. What is the main purpose of document 3?

a) To persuade
b) To inform
c) To instruct
d) To compare

13. Look at document 3. List 3 techniques that the write uses in order to enhance his or her message?

_____

_____

14. There is a spelling mistake in document 3. Can you spot it? Which 'word class' would the word come under?

_____

15. Look at document 3. What will individuals attending the training courses be able to achieve?

_____

Activity 2 – Produce an information sheet

You are a representative on a residents association. A local 'solar energy' company has approached several of the residents offering to install solar panels on the roofs of their houses (document 3).

Using documents 1, 2 and 3, produce an information sheet advising the residents of the issues they should consider in deciding whether or not to have solar panels installed on their roofs.

You may like to include:

• An introduction.

• A summary of the potential advantages and disadvantages of having solar panels installed on roofs.

• A conclusion, with some recommendations.

In your information sheet, you should also focus on writing clearly, accurate punctuation, grammar and spelling, and writing in paragraphs.

_____

_____

_____

_____

Activity 3 – Writing a letter

You notice a job advert in your local newspaper advertising several Trainee Apprenticeship positions at a new Alternative Energy Training Centre in Wales. Although the advert clearly states that no previous experience is necessary, it does state that a good work ethic is important, including punctuality and an eagerness to learn. It also states that good verbal and written communication skills are important along with a keen interest in issues relating to alternative energy.

Write a short letter of application (approximately one page) for the position of Trainee Apprentice to:

> Human Resources Manager
> Renewable Energy Centre
> Silverlink Way
> Cardiff
> South Glamorgan
> CF6 7JP

You should:

- Include a brief introduction.

- Let the company know why you are applying for the position.

- Let the company know why you feel that you are a suitable candidate for the position, and what you have to offer.

- Let the company know that you have enclosed your Curriculum Vitae.

- Let the company know that you look forward to hearing back from them.

- Focus on writing clearly, accurate punctuation, grammar and spelling, and writing in paragraphs.

_____

_____

_____

_____

_____

_____

_____

_____

_____

_____

_____

_____

_____

_____

_____

_____

_____

_____

_____

_____

_____

_____

Activity 4 – other renewable forms of energy

Using the internet, carry out some research into the following renewable
sources of energy:

a) Biomass

_____

_____

_____

_____

b) Hydroelectricity

_____

_____

_____

_____

_____

c) Geothermal Power

_____

_____

_____

_____

_____

d) Biofuels

_____

_____

_____

_____

_____

e) Fuel Cells

_____

_____

_____

_____

_____

Activity 5 – further research

There are plans in the future for wind farms to be used on a far larger scale than they currently are. It is anticipated that by 2020 for example, Britain will receive a quarter of all its energy through wind farms. Using the internet, carry out some research into the potential future use of wind farms. Consider issues such as their cost effectiveness and safety record:

_____

_____

Functional Skills - Writing

Young people have been gathering around your local parade of shops. According to the shopkeepers and local residents in the area, they frequently make a general nuisance of themselves by drinking, smoking, spitting and the casual use of bad language. In addition, local residents have complained that they feel intimidated by the youths and that they are afraid to walk through the area after dark.

Following several complaints, the council have proposed installing a sonic noise boom called the Mosquito, so called because it emits a buzzing noise of a particular frequency that only young people below the age of 25 can detect. The council have said that the Mosquito would only be activated after dark, near to the parade of shops, in order to deter the youths from congregating there. Questions have been raised in the local media however, as to whether or not such measures are ethical or, indeed, legal.

Activity 1 - Writing an email

As a local community youth worker, you are both sympathetic towards the concerns of local residents, and the frustrations of local youths who often complain that there is little for them to do in the area and nowhere else for them to congregate.

Write an email to your fellow community youth workers, the shop owners and members from the local residents association, inviting them to attend a meeting to discuss the issues.
In your email, you should:

- Outline where and when the meeting is due to take place and what the issues are that need to be discussed.

- Focus on writing clearly, accurate punctuation, grammar and spelling, and writing in paragraphs.

To:

Subject:

_____

_____

_____

_____

_____

_____

_____

_____

_____

_____

Activity 2 – Writing a letter

In preparation for the meeting, you decide that it would be a good idea to gain some information concerning the legal situation with regard to the installation of the Mosquito from a solicitor. With that in mind, write a letter to the solicitor outlining the issues involved and requesting advice. The name and address of the solicitor is: Mrs Brown, Hedges Solicitors Ltd, North Road, Rockford RF3 4AW

In your letter, you should also focus on writing clearly, accurate punctuation, grammar and spelling, and writing in paragraphs.

_____

_____

_____

_____

_____

_____

_____

_____

_____

Answers

Literacy Exercise (a)

The managers **were** surprised to **hear** about the theft. They were told that the thieves had broken into the hotel and stolen **their** keys. They **received** the news quite late at night. They were told that the thieves had been **given too many** opportunities to break in.

Have you ever had something stolen**?** If **you're planning** to make your house more secure, you should do so instantaneously!

Literacy Exercise (b)

The new asse**s**sor, who come**s** from the north of England**,** started work for the new company last Friday**. T**hroughout his first few days, he often asked himself why he'd come south to look for work in the first place. I'd heard him ask a col**l**eague, **"**Do you think life is so much better in the south**?"**

   "Not necessari**ly**" his colleague replied, "Don't dec**ei**ve yourself" he continued, "**A**sk for other people**'**s views but decide for yourself after you**'**ve lived here a while. There **are** a few clubs you could join to get to know some people. It **doesn't** really matter who you ask though, as everyone**'**s biased to some extent."

Capital Letters and Full Stops

1. **I** went to **B**righton last week and **I'**ll go there again tomorrow**.**
2. **M**y friend likes to keep fit**. H**e eats healthily and goes swimming most days of the week**.**
3. **S**he took longer than expected to reach the border, because the coach kept stopping**.**
4. **H**arry and **S**teve are flying to **B**erlin in **O**ctober**. T**hey'll stay there for about a week, then travel across to **B**ritain**.**
5. **G**eorge felt unwell during the conference, so left before the end**.**
6. **I** had bacon, eggs, tomatoes, beans and mushrooms for breakfast, so for lunch **I'**ll probably just have a tuna sandwich**.**
7. **H**e called the surgery to arrange a telephone appointment with one of the doctors**. D**r **J**ohn then called him sometime in the afternoon**.**
8. **T**here were lots of people at the party last night**. M**ost of them were new to the organisation**.**
9. **T**hey didn't really want to stay at the **S**heraton **H**otel, but at the end of the

day they didn't really have much choice**.**

10.**T**here were twenty five students in the classroom, all of whom were waiting to do their assessment**.**

11.**F**or lunch we had fishcakes, rice and vegetables**. L**ater, we had bread and butter pudding with custard for dessert**.**

12.**I**'ll never forget that adventure in **L**ake **M**alawi**. I**t's hard to believe that we were stuck in the mud when the flash storm started**.**

Apostrophes (to show belonging)

1. The assessors read through the learner**'**s portfolio.

2. The verifiers observed the assessors all afternoon.

3. I read the stories in last week**'**s newspaper.

4. He ran his family**'**s business like anyone else**'**s business.

5. My children**'**s ages are six and seven.

6. He was the people**'**s choice.

7. The men**'**s room is just around the corner.

8. The dog**'**s collar is red. It is wagging its tail.

9. He read his brother**'**s new book with great enthusiasm.

10. She receives her paycheques on a regular basis.

In the following sentences, underline the words which contain an apostrophe:

1. ****!*!--)** noun verb adverb -- !".:

2. ****!*!--)** adjective noun adjective noun -- !".:

3. ****!*!--)** noun noun verb adverb -- !".:

4. ****!*!--)** verb nouns adverb -- !".:

Look at these 4 sentences, then choose the correct answer below:

C) The apostrophe goes before the s in all of the above ('s).

Punctuation reading exercises
Exercise 1 (The Stockpot)

"Can I speak to the manager please**?" I** asked**,** rather nervously**,** having just finished my meal.

The restaurant's location in London's West End, combined with its friendly service and well-deserved reputation for serving reasonably priced food, made it an ideal place for meeting up with friends before a show. The menu offered mainly Anglo European cuisine consisting of traditional dual composites such as liver and bacon, fish and chips, apple crumble and custard, bubble and squeak, and jelly and ice cream etc.

"Sure, I'll tell him", she replied.

A minute or so later, after finishing making some drinks from behind the tiny bar, the manager walked the few yards across towards our table and gave me a slightly puzzled look. I'd been there enough times for him to recognise me as a regular customer and for me to recognise him as one of the managers.

"I've been coming here, and your other restaurants, for the past thirty years", I began, in a precise, deliberate tone, designed perhaps to maintain the manager's puzzled expression, "And have never had bad service", I continued, before pausing to maintain the suspense, "And I just wanted to say thank you!"

The manager remained perplexed for a moment or two, before breaking into a cautious, then more open, smile.

"We like to do the best for our customers", he eventually replied.

"Thanks again", I said, feeling slightly awkward.

"You're welcome", the manager replied.

Exercise 2 (The midwife)

After the phone call, the new midwife hastily put on her coat, grabbed her well-worn, leather bag of life delivery tools and, following a long, deep breath, hurried out into the cold, night air. She then climbed onto one of the many midwives' bicycles, which were parked up against the wall of the nunnery, and began cycling through the capital city's deserted streets of cobbled stones towards the nearby housing estate, where an expectant mother, and apprehensive father, anxiously awaited.

When she arrived, the midwife climbed the grey, grimy, concrete steps to the family's home, which was on the top floor of a block of flats. Throughout her first few days, she'd often asked herself why she'd taken up one of the most demanding jobs imaginable, but three hours and one screaming baby later, along with the look on the baby's mother's face, she realised that the midwife's job was a worthwhile one.

Exercise 3 (The engineer)

"Don't forget Latin America!" the tutor yelled, as I made my way hurriedly from the classroom.

"I won't" I replied, slowing down with a feeling of guilt that I was rushing to get away.

I'd wanted to stay. **A**fter all, during the break, some in the group had suggested that, as it was the last night of the **L**atin **A**merican **S**tudies course, we should all go out for a drink. **I**'d made some good acquaintances on the course too. **I** remember one of the guys from the group had asked me what my job was.

"**I'm** a civil engineer" **I**'d said.

"I am a fugitive from a chain gang" he'd replied, to my utter amazement. **H**e'd seen the film on the telly the previous week, he went on to say. **I**'d seen it too, but then **I** was a civil engineer and had waited for the film with excited anticipation as it was, to my knowledge, the only film until then that had been made about one. **I**t was a 1930s black and white **H**ollywood film about a civil engineer who, as a wrongfully convicted convict on a chain gang, puts up with intolerable conditions before escaping to **C**hicago. **T**hrough his relationships, his time on the chain gang come back to haunt him. **I**'d seen it on a small portable black and white **TV** in a pokey, little, run down bedsit off the **K**ings Road in **F**ulham.

Grammar Exercise

The organisers could have run the project themselves. After all, it was their idea. However, most of them **were** probably too inexperienced, and couldn't have known everything that was involved in managing such a large project or how much it would cost.

Although the sports council had given plenty of money for similar ideas in the past, last year they only **gave** a small amount towards their project. Following this, the organisers weren't able to get **any** be equipment, and therefore many of the training sessions had to be cancelled. As a result, the clients **stopped** coming to the centre and instead began using the facilities at the nearby business park. Problems then seemed to come their way from all directions. The organisers could have guessed what was likely to happen, but it wasn't until the letters started arriving in the post that they could finally **see** the extent of their problems. When the director of the sports council **came** to see them at their office early one morning, they knew that their project was nearing the end of its time.

More or Less?

The sign should read 'about 20 items or **fewer**', because the number of items can be counted. We use 'less' for non-countable nouns and 'fewer' for countable nouns.

For example:

There were fewer crimes committed last year (you can count the number of crimes).

There was less crime committed last year (you cannot count crime).

There were less people at the station this morning (this is incorrect as you can count the number of people. It should be 'There were fewer people at the station this morning').

Letters

Formal letter of complaint

26 Burley Rd
Hayford
West Yorkshire
HY2 4ET

February 17th 2012

The Manager
Morsco Supemarket
Market Square
Hayford HY3 2SD

Dear Sir or Madam

I am writing to complain about the standard of **service** that I received in your supermarket yesterday evening. I decided to try out the new self-service checkouts, which you have recently had installed, in order to check out **their effectiveness**. **Unfortunately** however, the machine didn't seem to be working **properly** and an annoying**,** automated voice kept saying**,** "**Please** remove unwanted items in the bagging area!" Each time this happened, I had to call for assistance and wait for what seemed like ages for someone to come and sort the problem out. Who knows, maybe I need more **practice**?

I wouldn't **have** minded having to wait for so long if the supermarket had **actually** been busy, but each time the store **assistant** arrived to sort out the problem, he became more and more abrupt. Furthermore, he failed to apologise for keeping me waiting. I hope that by the time I visit your store next, that you will have either had the **opportunity** to improve the self-service checkouts or the customer service standards of your shop **assistants**!

Yours **faithfully**

Kevin Norley

Formal letter of enquiry

18 Caversham Street
Fersham Green
Rutland
FS2 8JR

February 17th, 2012

Mr Dean
Mercury Leisure Centre
Fersham Green
Rutland FS1 0QT

Dear Mr Dean

A **colleague** of mine has recently informed me that there may be new Zumba and Capoeira classes starting at the Mercury **Leisure** Centre in the new year. I would **appreciate** it if you could provide me with details of the classes i.e. the time and date and cost etc. In addition, I would be **grateful** if you could send me details of other fitness classes that you run, and any **brochures** or leaflets you may have concerning the cost of **leisure centre**, and gym, membership etc.

   From what I can understand, there will be **fewer children's** swimming classes at the leisure centre next year, due to the local **contractor's** on-going **maintenance** work occurring at the centre. If that is so, could you please let me know which classes will still be running, and when the full **schedule** of swimming classes are likely to return to normal.

   I look forward to hearing from you.

Yours **sincerely**

Kevin Norley

Formal letter of thanks

84 Crossfield Rd
Tottenham
London
N14 4UR

February 10th, 2012

The manager
Hotpot Restaurant
Orange Bear St (off Leicester Square)
London
WC1

Dear Madam

On Wednesday evening, my friends and I enjoyed a really good **performance** of the new Billy Elliot musical at a theatre in the West End. Before the play started, we decided to go for a meal in the Leicester Square area. We didn't have a lot of time, so I **recommended** to them that we should go to the Hotpot. We didn't have a lot of money either, not after **'forking out'** so much for our theatre tickets anyway. Even though your restaurant was clearly very busy, you found us a table quite quickly after just a short wait. The service was then **excellent**; your **waiters** and waitresses **were** polite, efficient and friendly. The food was very good and, considering **it's** the West End, very reasonably priced.

   My friends have told me that when they go to the theatre again, either with other people, or again with me, they will try more dishes from your traditional menu of Anglo European cuisine. I would also like to add that I have been coming to your restaurant, and **its** sister restaurant, The West End Diner, for several years now and have always, without **exception**, enjoyed really good service and really good food!

   Thank you again.

Yours faithfully

Kevin Norley

Formal letter of application

26 The Link
Cardiff
South Glamorgan
CF1 2EP

February 10th, 2012

Mrs J Griffiths
Human Resources Manager
Renewable Energy Centre
Silverlink Way
Cardiff
South Glamorgan
CF6 7JP

Dear Mrs Griffiths

Further to your recent job **advertisement** in the Cardiff Chronicle, dated 7th June 2011, I am applying for the position of trainee energy **apprentice**.

As you can see from my CV, I have recent **voluntary** work experience. This provided me with the opportunity to become **familiar** with dealing with **customers** on a daily basis, and **allowed** me to become **accustomed** to having a daily work routine. As you can also see from my CV, I have recently **achieved** a level 2 qualification in adult literacy and a level 1 qualification in adult numeracy, and am currently working towards my level 2 at Barnford **College**.

I have good communication skills and am IT literate. I am reliable, keen and willing to learn new skills, and to undergo any training that is **necessary** for the job **role**. I have read about your company and the training that your **apprenticeship** programme offers, and believe that my skills and experience, combined with a high level of motivation, make me a **suitable** candidate for the position.

I enclose a CV for your perusal and look forward to hearing from you in due course.

Yours sincerely

Kevin Norley

Formal letter of apology

17 Oxford Rd
Newminster
Suffolk
NM3 4TY

February 10th, 2012

Mr Haleem
Urnsford College of Further Education
Newminster
Suffolk
NM2 1JP

Dear Mr **Haleem**

I wish to inform you that **unfortunately** I shall no longer be able to attend the **Complementary** Therapies course at the **college**. This is **dew** to the fact that my work **commitments** have increased over the past few weeks which, combined with my family obligations, means that I will no longer be able to attend all my sessions and complete the **necessary** coursework.

   I would like to apologise for any **inconvenience** that my withdrawal may cause and to take this opportunity to let you know that I have enjoyed your classes, **particularly t**he anatomy and **physiology** ones, and to thank you for having taught me over the past term. I have learnt a lot about the different types of **complementary** therapy treatments and experienced directly many of their **therapeutic** effects.

   I would also like to let you know that if my situation changes over the next few months, that I shall consider **re-enrolling** in **September**, during the next academic year.

Yours sincerely

Kevin Norley

English as an Additional Language (EAL)
English for Speakers of other Languages (ESOL)

When reflecting upon the literacy and language skills of people within the country, the needs of the country's large, and increasing, immigrant community has also, naturally, to be considered. The question here that needs to be asked is, 'How does the learning experience differ for the learner who is an EAL learner from that of an English native learner developing his/her literacy skills?'

A native learner acquires the English language from a very early age, whereas an EAL learner needs to learn the language. Hawkins (1984), in contrasting mother tongue learning during infancy and foreign language learning during school, argues that the motivation for mother tongue learning is greater than for foreign language learning because there is more in the way of discovery, excitement and associated rewards. Amongst EAL learners, Wallace (1988: 4&5) outlines the difference between those 'who are learning English as a foreign rather than a second language, and have come to Britain usually specifically to improve their English' and those from 'linguistic minorities who have settled in Britain' and who 'are likely to have to function in daily life, work and education primarily through the medium of English'.

The ability of an EAL adult learner to develop their literacy skills will depend on a variety of factors including their native language literacy skills (which in turn is a reflection of their educational background), personal circumstances and degree of motivation i.e. to what degree the learners need English in their daily lives e.g. work-related reasons, integration into the community, functional reasons (going to the doctor etc.) and the amount of exposure they get to the English language in their daily lives. Wallace (1988: 3) explains that for teachers of adult literacy, functional literacy should be the goal for their learners i.e. to be aware that it's 'part of everyday life in a personal and social sense'. However, she also argues that the degree to which EAL learners, who have a different first language and culture to that of the indigenous population, need and view literacy in their everyday lives depends on their social role within their community, and backs this up by giving examples of the varying literacy expectations on an Indian housewife and a Pakistani Muslim boy.

Amongst EAL learners, naturally the range of initial levels of acquisition can be quite vast i.e. from someone who has little or no knowledge of the English language and little experience of its usage, to someone who is nearly fluent.

Furthermore, there will be a wide ability range in terms of the learners' potential to develop their English literacy skills within such a range of learners. Common learning difficulties which EAL learners experience, whatever their starting point, relate to the degree to which the phonological system and grammatical structure of their own language differ from the English language. Common errors in spoken English amongst EAL learners relate to learners translating directly from their own language into English (mother tongue interference), using their native language's grammatical structures. However, the EAL learner may have strong literacy skills in their other language(s) and these are transferable but less so if the other languages use a different phonological system, and are written in scripts other than the Latin. If the first language is written in a non alphabetic script, even less so.

In comparing and contrasting the issues faced by native and non-native speakers in learning to read, Wallace (1988:64) argues that since native speakers use the English language in their daily lives and have an 'intuitive knowledge about their own language', then 'reading is not an alien code', whereas for non-native speakers, they have to use 'what they know of English to predict the structure and vocabulary of written English' and as such may have, depending on their English competence, 'difficulty in anticipating certain structures in written texts'. Furthermore, Carrell (1987) points out that amongst adults, research has shown that:

> When a reader and writer share cultural assumptions and knowledge about social systems and rituals, there is a much higher level of interaction of the reader with the text than occurs when such assumptions and knowledge are not shared.

> **(Carrell 1987: 43)**

An EAL learner's native language literacy skills will also affect their English reading skills in that if they have, for example, a poor comprehension of punctuation, or a sound knowledge of punctuation conventions in the first language which are not the same as those of English, then this will serve as an additional barrier in reading to the understanding of text to that served by understanding of vocabulary and pronunciation of words; and similarly for writing, poor handwriting skills and/or a poor comprehension of punctuation, grammar and spelling rules in the EAL learner's own language will compound a learner's difficulties in writing in another language.

Native learners who wish to develop their literacy skills however, are less likely to be concerned with English language usage, but more concerned with developing their reading and writing skills. The literacy skills which need to be developed, will naturally relate (as with EAL learners) to the level of literacy skills which the native learner already has. Those skills will, in turn, relate to the learners' own educational experiences and socio-economic background, abilities and interest. The incentives for the native learner to improve their literacy skills will naturally relate to their own motivation and personal and work-related circumstances.

EAL learners are less likely to be aware of the range of non-standard English dialects that exist in the United Kingdom than a native learner, and as such, would need to be exposed during learning sessions to a range of dialects. Native learners on the other hand, who use non-standard dialects may not be aware of grammatical errors that they make in their spoken English (e.g. use of you was, 'you was', 'I done' and 'we haven't got no' etc. are all quite common in non-standard dialects), and how this may impact on their written English. Also, it should be considered that there will be many EAL learners who, due to the areas they live in, may be equally, or more likely, to accept the non-standard colloquialisms around them as standard (e.g. 'innit?').

In the early stages of literacy where a sound-letter correspondence is being taught, care should be taken to ensure that the learner has an opportunity to hear the sound. Materials intended for native speakers often assume a knowledge of vocabulary (e.g. a picture of an igloo next to the letter I), but this knowledge cannot be assumed for EAL learners. When teaching vocabulary, the meaning, spoken form of the word, and written form of the word should all be emphasised with an EAL learner. If lessons are tailored to the needs of native learners, there is a possibility of neglecting one or other of the first two. Generally speaking, EAL learners will have a smaller vocabulary, and less of an instinctive knowledge of collocation (words that go with other words) e.g. traffic jam, traffic lights, draconian measures. A strategy employed by successful readers, that of guessing from context, cannot be employed by them unless the teacher ensures that there are not too many gaps in the text i.e. limits the vocabulary load. Writing frames, prepared for a range of levels, can be a useful strategy for developing writing skills in both EAL and native learners. Examples of writing frames (writing letters, applying for courses etc.) can be found in Writing Works (2001). Both EAL and native learners could benefit from the support of pictures.

EAL learners will want to advance their knowledge of the English language alongside their literacy skills (acquiring new vocabulary and structures). In supporting general English acquisition through the written and spoken word, teachers should avoid the danger of overloading the text with unknowns and thus sabotaging the developing literacy skills. It should also be borne in mind that EAL learners who have advanced literacy skills in their own language may feel insulted by the simplicity of the content of beginner's texts. Similar sensitivity is required with adult native speakers too, as they tend not to want to read childish texts. Furthermore, EAL learners who do read well in their other language(s) should be explicitly taught how to use a bilingual dictionary.

When reflecting on theories of language and development in order to choose an approach that would best enable any given learner to develop their literacy skills, it can be considered that according to Knowles (1998: 22), 'Learning theories fall into two major families: *behaviourist/connectionist theories* and *cognitive/gestalt theories*' Whereas cognitive development theories relate to understanding why adult learners have difficulties in dealing with quite advanced issues (Knowles 1998), behaviourist theories are based on the idea that learning is a function of change in overt behaviour and that those changes are the result of an individual's response to events (stimuli) that occur in the environment. The theory, as applied to language development, centres around the idea that a stimulus (such as the first sentence of a dialogue) meets with a response and that if that stimulus and response is praised or rewarded by the teacher, a stimulus-response pattern can be established with a learner which conditions that particular learner to respond in future instances. Reinforcement is the key element in the stimulus-response theory, where the reinforcement is anything that strengthens the desired response e.g. verbal praise, a good grade etc.

For a learner who is illiterate, language practice should take the form of question (stimulus) and answer (response) frames which expose students to the language in gradual steps. This requires that the learner makes a response for every frame and receives immediate feedback in the form of positive reinforcement on the basis that behaviour that is positively reinforced will reoccur. If a learner is illiterate, it is likely that they will have arrived in the UK as an immigrant or refugee from a rural community within a developing country (in Africa or Asia) where literacy is not as highly valued as it would be in other types of community. As such, there is a likelihood that the learner will have come from a tradition where although oral fluency would be important, literacy skills such as reading and writing are less valued, particularly for women. Furthermore, if a learner is illiterate in their own language, it is likely that their language skills will have been acquired in an informal way rather than learnt in a formal manner. Krashen (1981) outlines the difference between 'language acquisition' (the natural assimilation of language rules through using language for communication) and 'language learning' (the formal study of language rules as a conscious process).

In terms of theories of language learning, an approach which could be considered for an illiterate learner is the 'interactional view', whereby according to Richards and Rodgers (2001: 21), language is seen 'as a vehicle for the realization of interpersonal relations and for the performance of social transactions between individuals' and therefore 'as a tool for the creation and maintenance of social relations'.

An illiterate person will initially need the native language to 'survive' in a community i.e. to be able to interact with others in carrying out everyday functions such as shopping, accessing services and finding a job etc. It is important therefore that learning reflects realistic everyday life situations. In discussing adult learning theory, Knowles (1998) states that:

'Adults are motivated to learn as they experience needs and interests that learning will satisfy' and that 'Adults orientation to learning is life-centred; therefore, the appropriate units for organising adult learning are life situations, not subjects.

(Knowles 1998: 40)

In distinguishing between theories of learning and theories of teaching, Gagne (1985) has argued that while learning theories address methods of learning, teaching theories address the methods employed to influence learning.

An example of such a method, which is based on the learning theory of behaviourism (discussed above) is the 'audio-lingual method'. According to Harmer (1991: 32), the method makes 'constant drilling of the students followed by positive or negative reinforcement a major focus of classroom activity'. Basing the methodology on the stimulus-response-reinforcement model, mistakes are, according to Harmer (1991: 32) 'immediately criticised, and correct utterances … immediately praised.'

Other teaching methodologies focus more on the humanistic aspects of learning, whereby it is argued that language teaching should, in focusing on learners' experiences, look to develop themselves as people and encourage positive feelings (Harmer 1991). Advocates of humanistic approaches then would, according to Harmer (1991: 36) tend to use classroom activities that made learners 'feel good and … remember happy times and events whilst at the same time practising language'. In terms of classroom activities that could be used to develop an illiterate learner's aural skills, it should be borne in mind that, according to Ur (1984: 35), 'a grasp of the phonology of the new language is a fairly basic requisite for learning to speak it' and also a prerequisite for later developing sound-written symbol relationships. With this in mind, she advocates listening exercises whereby the learner is given the opportunity to practise 'identifying correctly different sounds, sound-combinations and intonations'.

In order that the focus will be predominantly on developing the learner's aural perception skills, Ur (1984: 35) suggests minimising visual stimuli and 'contextual clues to meaning' through use of a range of recordings rather than live speech. At the word level then, the learner practises listening to and repeating words in isolation from each other. Time should be built into the activities by the teacher for error correction and positive feedback to the learner.

At sentence level however, the difficulties for a learner increases as aural perception is hampered by the idiosyncrasies of English speech, such as word contractions, unstressed syllables, elision of consonants and variation in vowel sounds. In order to further develop the learner's aural skills, activities need now to be focused on sensitising the learner to the 'blurring' of words that takes place in spoken discourse due to the above. The learner needs to listen to and repeat short phrases or sentences, still ensuring, as above, that they rely predominantly on their ear. Further aural activities can include; listening to recordings of short sentences and answering the question, 'how many words?', and listening to recordings of short sentences and asking if certain facts are true or false. Care should be taken to ensure that there is not too much in the way of new language or utterances introduced into each session that may 'overload' the learner, and that time is allowed for continual error correction and feedback to the learner.

On the basis that both the above activities rely on a stimulus (the learner hearing words or sentences) and a response (repetition of the word or sentence), error correction, drilling and positive reinforcement, I would argue that they lend themselves towards the audio-lingual teaching method and are hence based on a behaviourist learning model.

I have spent the past few years teaching ESOL part-time in evening classes to adult students in an inner-city college. The students come from a variety of backgrounds, the majority coming from countries across the Asian sub-continent and eastern Europe. Naturally, any group of learners starting a class will come from a variety of backgrounds and be motivated to learn English through a mixture of intrinsic and extrinsic factors. As such, the learners within a class will vary in their ability to learn. As far as it is possible, learners are banded together in a class following an initial assessment of their speaking and listening, reading and writing skills, against criteria relating to a given level. Most are at entry 2 or entry 3 level, are literate in their own language and have been living in the country from a few months to a few years (although some have been living here for many years). The individual learners (and the classes as a whole) have always been exceptionally courteous, making them a pleasure to teach. I often encourage and nag my classes to engage more in the English language i.e. to read as wide a range of texts as possible and to practise speaking the language with people outside of the college. One thing I reflect on however is the lack of pressure exerted on them by society in general and employers in particular to improve their language skills. This I believe is a factor in preventing many ESOL learners from integrating fully into British communities.

A widely discussed and contentious 'hot topic' that is frequently on the News is the issue of immigration and how it may, or may not, affect the employment prospects of British born people. So, I was returning to my car following a shopping trip to IKEA when I found a young guy fiddling with the wheel nuts on my car. When I asked if I could help him, he became a little agitated, muttered some expletives in an aggressive manner and local accent, and wondered off. Not wanting to let him just get away with it, I approached a guy wearing a yellow fluorescent jacket, whom I'd assumed to be a security guard. He was indeed a security guard, and some security firm's employee, but when I began telling him about what had happened, he looked somewhat blank and replied in very broken English; judging by his accent and appearance, I guessed he was of East African origin. I didn't see the point of engaging the guy further in trying to make him understand what the issue was, so went back to my car and drove off. People act and think depending on their own experiences, and I felt a sense of isolation, in a small part, based on the needless and worthless experience itself with the two guys amidst the thousands of shoppers, but more from my reflections on the incident. As I was driving out of the car park, I noticed the guy was trying to unscrew the wheel nuts from some other poor git!

Once I'd driven far enough away, and with the certainty that no more related experiences were to be had there, the thoughts began to kick in, queuing up and vying for my attention! First up was the annoying question of what had led to a young, apparently physically fit, young man to have nothing better to do than to spend his time trying to nick the wheel nuts from cars. Secondly, I wondered why it was that a security guard was employed, who was not able to converse properly in English (as they sometimes are, I've noticed, in other environments such as large supermarkets) and consequently not able to assist me. Two commonly expressed views then sprang to mind both of which relate more to the fate of the working class in this country, but neither of which are held by myself; 'Immigrants are coming over here and taking our jobs!' and 'British people are too lazy to do many jobs!', the former being more commonly expressed by those of working class background and the latter, of middle class.

When I previously taught English to Speakers of other Languages in inner-city areas to immigrants living here, I used to sometimes wonder how it was that in spite of having quite a basic command of the language, many of my students, particularly, but not only, those from the Asian Subcontinent (well, the men anyway, since many females from the Asian Subcontinent were restricted in their opportunities due to cultural, and child care constraints) could quite readily find employment in areas such as the hotel industry, catering, security and picking and packing etc. It would seem fair to me if employers (both from the private and public sector) were to stipulate, as a condition of employment, the ability to speak English fluently. This should give a fair advantage to native speakers in the employment stakes, and within that context, put pressure on them to take up available jobs and in so doing, test the afore-mentioned adage. The onus then would be placed on non-native speakers to engage in and learn the English language which in turn would assist them in integrating more into British society, and in so doing halting the ever-increasing ghettoisation of British society.

If we were to add to this mix an obligation for employers to require their potential employees (excluding those with specific, diagnosed learning disabilities) to be able to demonstrate basic literacy skills too, then this would add another dimension, giving fair advantage to those with basic literacy skills, placing the onus on those without these skills to obtain them, such that they can engage more in, and play a greater role within, their own country's culture and provide themselves with greater opportunities within the job market. Employers are, after all, reporting time and again that based on the CVs they look at, so many are failing to put a sentence together. Pressure would then need to be put on those responsible for young people's education, from Government policy makers to classroom teachers, to ensure that they obtain those necessary skills.

Arguments could, and probably would however, be put forward along the lines of, 'What do people doing particular types of manual or service sector work need language and/or literacy skills for?' Whether or not such questions are overtly expressed, the fact is that in general, it is those who lack language and literacy skills who are in greatest competition for work and resources, supplying the needs of a society hooked on preserving social class through political organisations, businesses, educational institutions and of course that old chestnut, human nature!

I often begin classes by focusing on common, everyday questions and answers, and expressions, that the learner is likely to be familiar with, and which do not require any broad knowledge of grammar or tenses, such as, 'How are you?', 'What is your name?', 'What time is it?' and 'Where are your from?' etc By restricting the variation in the grammar within the questions and answers to the components of the verb 'to be', a tutor is able to focus on developing their learners' fluency.

For example, students should get used to the sound of contractions early on, and be given the opportunity to practise listening and responding to questions with them. As well as being encouraged to use contractions in speech, they should learn how to recognise and write with (and without) them.

Attention should also be paid at this stage to the pronunciation of unstressed syllables in speech, as a means of improving learners' fluency. Due to the nature of English as a 'stress-timed' language, it is common for an ESOL learner to miss out or 'pass over' unstressed syllables such as 'a', 'the', ''m', 'are' and 'to'. The location and importance of these syllables can be reinforced through reading and writing exercises which clearly highlight the position of the unstressed syllables.

Present tense (everyday questions)

How **are** you?   I **am** fine thanks   I**'m** fine thanks
What **is** your name?   What**'s** your name?   My name **is**...   My name's…
What **is** his name?   What**'s** his name?   His name **is**…   His name**'s**…
Where **are** you from?   I **am** from…   I**'m** from…
Where **is** he from?   Where**'s** he from?   He **is** from…   He**'s** from…
Where **is** she from?   Where**'s** she from?   She **is** from…   She**'s** from …
Where **are** they from?   They **are** from …
What time **is** it?   It **is** ten past eight.   It**'s** ten past eight.
What **is** the date today?   It **is** the 12th of July
What**'s** the date today?   It**'s** the 22nd of August
What **is** your job?   I **am** a…
What**'s** your job?   I**'m** a…
How old **are** you?   I **am** 26 years old.   I**'m** 26 years old.
Where**'s** the pen?   It**'s** on the desk.
Where **are** the pens?   They **are** on the desk.
Where**'s** the book?   It**'s** on the shelf

Where**'s** the nearest toilet please? It**'s** down the corridor on the right.
Is there a supermarket nearby? Yes, there**'s** one in the centre of town.
Are there many people in town today? Yes there **are** (many people in town today). No there **aren't** (many people in town today).
Are there any mountains in your country? Yes there **are** (mountains in my country).
No there **aren't** (any mountains in my country). Etc

The verb used to form the above sentences is, **'To Be'** which is:

I am	We are (Kate and I are)
You are (s)	You are (pl)
He is (Fred is)	They are (James and Sarah are)
She is (Jane is)	
It is (The car is; My idea is; etc)	

The verb also needs to be known in its negative, interrogative and negative interrogative forms:

I am not (= I'm not)
You are not (s) (= you're not or
    you aren't)
He is not (= he's not or he isn't)
She is not (= she's not or she isn't)
It is not (= it's not or it isn't)

We are not (= we're not or
    we aren't)
You are not (pl) (= you're not or
    you aren't)
They are not (= they're not or
    they aren't)

Am I?
Are you? (s)
Is he? (Is Fred?)
Is she? (Is she?)
Is it (Is the car?)

Are we? (Are Kate and I?)
Are you? (pl)
Are they? (Are James and Sarah?)

Are we not? (Aren't we?)
Are you not? (pl) (= Aren't you?)
Are they not? (Aren't they?)

Am I not?
Are you not? (s) (= Aren't you?)
Is he not? (Isn't he?)
Is she not? (Isn't she?)
Is it not? (Isn't it?)

In the above, there isn't much change in the grammatical structure, but there is room to increase vocabulary (e.g. objects around the room, or professions) in degrees appropriate to the abilities of the students within the class.

On the basis that many learners will not necessarily have the level of English to understand explanations regarding tenses, they will need to be demonstrated, and learnt through use i.e. combining speaking and listening, reading and writing exercises. Use of tenses can be learnt in the context of comparing the use of one tense in relation to another. For example, the present continuous can be explained through illustrating what is happening at the present moment ('now') or through describing momentary, or temporary, actions. This can be compared and contrasted with the simple present, which can be explained through illustrating events that happen all the time or sometimes, or that are true in general. The use of the present continuous in describing momentary actions, can be illustrated through pictures, such as in the following examples, then compared and contrasted with the use of the simple present:

Look at the pictures below.

1

2

3

4

Picture **1** (present continuous):
What's he do**ing**? He's teach**ing**.

Picture **2** (present continuous):
What's she do**ing**? She's work**ing** on the computer.

Picture **3** (present continuous):
What are they do**ing**? They're hav**ing** a meeting.

Picture 4 (present continuous):
Is it rain**ing** outside? Yes it is (rain**ing** outside).

The present simple:

1. He teaches part-time in the college.
2. She works on the computer every day.
3. They have a meeting every Thursday afternoon.
4. It usually rains in Autumn.

A way of further helping students to distinguish between the use of these 'paired' tenses, can be to highlight how the use of the subject and verb in the answer reflects the question. A common mistake made by ESOL learners in their spoken English is to omit the verb 'to be' from the present continuous, for example, *'I going to town later.'* Naturally, in the context of delivering learning in an ESOL class, such errors should be constantly and consistently corrected, and the proper use of the present continuous reinforced through structured written exercises. The exercise on page .. (Correcting mistakes made in everyday spoken English) for example, gives learners the opportunity to identify and correct such errors (in spoken and written English).

Present continuous Vs Present simple

Present Continuous

What <u>are you</u> do**ing** now?
<u>I'm</u> learn**ing** English; <u>I'm</u> sitt**ing** down; <u>I'm</u> read**ing** a newspaper; <u>I'm</u> looking at the board; <u>I'm</u> listening to music; <u>I'm</u> working on the computer.

<u>What's Abdul</u> do**ing**?
<u>He's</u> learn**ing** English; <u>He's</u> play**ing** football; <u>He's</u> play**ing** on the computer.

<u>What's he</u> do**ing**?
<u>He's</u> learn**ing** English; <u>He's</u> watch**ing** TV; <u>He is</u> fill**ing** in an application form.

What <u>are they</u> do**ing**?
<u>They are</u> play**ing** cricket; <u>They're</u> go**ing** shopping; <u>They're</u> walk**ing** home.

<u>Is the computer</u> work**ing**?
Yes, <u>it is</u> (work**ing**). No, <u>it isn't</u> (work**ing**).

<u>Are the trains</u> running on time?
Yes, <u>they are</u> (running on time). No, <u>they're not</u> (runn**ing** on time). Etc

Present simple

Where <u>do you work?</u> <u>I work</u> in Milton Keynes.

Where <u>does he work?</u> <u>He works</u> in Milton Keynes

Where <u>does John work?</u> <u>He works</u> in Milton Keynes.

What time <u>do you get up</u> in the morning? <u>I</u> usually <u>get up</u> at half past seven.

What time <u>does she get up</u> in the morning? <u>She gets up</u> at half past seven.

What time <u>does Helen get up</u> in the morning? <u>She gets up</u> at half past seven.

Do you like coffee? Yes, **I do** (like coffee). No, **I don't** (like coffee).

Does he take milk and sugar? Yes, **he does**. No, he doesn't.

Do they go there often? Yes, **they do**. No, **they don't**. Etc.

The verb that needs to be learnt in the context of the above tense is 'to do', as an auxiliary (or supplementary) verb, including in its negative, interrogative and negative interrogative forms, since its structure, in each of these forms, can frequently cause difficulties with ESOL learners. A common error with the third person singular interrogative for example is to use the 's' ending twice e.g. Does he likes his present? The exercise on P84 (correcting mistakes made in everyday spoken English) includes examples whereby such errors can be identified and corrected (in spoken and written English).

To do

I do	We do (Paul and I do)
You do (s)	You do (pl)
He does (Michael does)	They do (Johanna and Graham do)
She does (Sarah does)	
It does (The car does)	

I don't	We don't (Paul and I don't)
You don't (s)	You don't (pl)
He doesn't (Michael doesn't)	They don't (Johanna and Graham don't)
She doesn't (Sarah doesn't)	
It doesn't (The car doesn't)	
Do I?	Do we? (Do Paul and I?)
Do you? (s)	Do you? (pl)
Does he? (Does Michael?)	Do they? (Do Johanna and Graham?)
Does she? (Does Sarah?)	
Does it? (Does the car?)	

Don't I?	Don't we? (Do Paul and I?)
Don't you? (s)	Don't you? (pl)
Doesn't he? (Does Michael?)	Don't they? (Do Johanna and Graham?)
Doesn't she? (Does Sarah?)	
Doesn't it? (Doesn't the car?)	

Throughout the learners' learning process, the tutor should ensure constant and consistent correction of errors, such as those indicated above related to developing their learners' fluency and pronunciation generally. If, as is commonly the case with students developing their spoken English skills, they find themselves hesitating or pausing between particular words in a sentence which do not require a pause, then a line (/) can be put through the written sentence on the board to indicate where the hesitation is occurring. When this has been done, the learner can be given the opportunity to practise blending the two relevant syllables either side of the pause. This procedure can further help develop learners' fluency.

Present continuous Vs Past continuous

Here, the use of the **present continuous** can be elaborated on and developed to include the future. This can be best explained through linking its use with a time reference, for example:

What are you do**ing** tomorrow? I'm work**ing** all day; **I'm** go**ing to** town;

I'm going shopp**ing**; **I'm** visit**ing** my friend

When are you go**ing to** Pakistan? We**'re** go**ing** there in the summer;

When **is** he start**ing** his course? He**'s** starting **it** next week;

What**'s** she do**ing** later? She**'s** go**ing to** the theatre. Etc.

This can be compared with the use of the **past continuous**, which can be explained in the context of putting across the idea that you are describing a continuous action that was happening in the past. For example:

What <u>were you</u> do**ing** yesterday afternoon?

<u>I was</u> work**ing**. I was watch**ing** TV

What <u>were they</u> do**ing** yesterday evening?

<u>They were</u> work**ing**. <u>They were</u> watch**ing** TV.

Where <u>was she</u> go**ing** earlier?

<u>She was</u> go**ing** into town. <u>She was</u> go**ing** to the library.

Who <u>was Colin</u> meet**ing** last night?

<u>He was</u> meet**ing** his girlfriend. <u>He was</u> meet**ing** his colleagues. Etc.

Again, the use of the verb in the answer can be shown to reflect its use in the question. The past continuous can be further illustrated through its use after 'while' and 'when'. For example:

'While I was cooking, I burnt myself.'

'I saw you when you were swimming.'

'She called while I was sleeping.'

'They arrived while I was taking a shower.'

As with the present continuous, a common error made by ESOL learners using the past continuous is to omit the verb 'to be', for example, *'I working yesterday.'* As with errors made in the use of the present continuous, errors made in the use of the past continuous should be constantly and consistently corrected, and its proper use reinforced through structured written exercises.

Past continuous Vs Simple past

In order to explain the use of the **simple past**, you can put across the idea that you are describing an action that has been completed, and compared with the above for the past continuous. For example:

What **did you do** yesterday afternoon? **I went** to the cinema.
I went shopping.

What **did Jean do** yesterday afternoon?

She went to the cinema. **She went** shopping.

Where **did you have** lunch? **I had** it in the school canteen.

What **did you have** for lunch?

I had fried chicken and chips. **I had** a lasagne with a salad.

What **did she have** for lunch?

She had fried chicken and chips. **She had** a lasagne with a salad.

Who **did you see** at school this morning?

I saw the headmaster. **I saw** my son's form teacher.

Who **did he see** at school this morning?

He saw the headmaster. **He saw** his son's form teacher.

Did you go out last night?

Yes **I did** (go out last night). No **I didn't** (go out last night).

Did she collect her car? Yes **she did**. No **she didn't**.

Did he meet his friend? Yes **he did**. No **he didn't**.

Did they win the match? Yes **they did**. No **they didn't**. Etc

Common errors in the use of the simple past, include using the past form twice, for example:

'Did you saw him?'

'I didn't went to the cinema.'

Past simple Vs Present perfect

The use of the **present perfect** (have + past participle) can be explained in the context of describing an event which has finished in the recent past (or is unfinished), whereas with the simple past, there is a specific time reference, for example: last week, yesterday, in April 1994, a month ago etc. With the present perfect, we often use the following time adverbials: yet, already, recently, just, never, lately, ever etc.

> **Have you** ever **been** to America? Yes *or* Yes, I have
> (*means* yes, **I have been** to America).

> **Have you heard of** John Lennon? No *or* No, I haven't
> (*means* no, **I haven't heard of** John Lennon).

> I have never eaten marmite. *c.f.* I ate marmite last week.
> She has just arrived. *c.f.* She arrived at 3 o'clock.

> We have never been to Paris.
> I have lived in England for 3 years.
> We have known each other for 2 weeks.
> He has worked there since September.
> I have already told you.
> She has already eaten.
> We have not finished yet.

The verb that needs to be learnt in the context of the above tense is 'to have', as an auxiliary (or supplementary) verb, including in its negative, interrogative and negative interrogative forms as its structure, in each of these forms, can frequently cause difficulties with ESOL learners:

To have

I have	We have (Paul and I have)
You have (s)	You have (pl)
He has (Michael has)	They have (Johanna and Graham have)
She has (Sarah has)	
It has (The computer has)	

I haven't	We haven't (Paul and I haven't)
You haven't (s)	You haven't (pl)
He hasn't (Michael hasn't)	They haven't (Johanna and Graham haven't)
She hasn't (Sarah hasn't)	
It hasn't (The computer hasn't)	

Have I?	Have we? (Have Paul and I?)
Have you? (s)	Have you? (pl)
Has he? (Has Michael?)	Have they (Have Johanna and Graham?)
Has she? (Has Sarah?)	
Has it? (Has the computer?)	

Haven't I?	Haven't we? (Haven't Paul and I?)
Haven't you? (s)	Haven't you? (pl)
Hasn't he? (Hasn't Michael?)	Haven't they (Haven't Johanna and Graham?)
Hasn't she? (Hasn't Sarah?)	
Hasn't it? (Hasn't the computer?)	

I have found over the years, that even for ESOL speakers who have been living in the UK for several years, and who have good jobs here, that it's the distinction between the use of the past simple and present perfect that is often the hardest, and one of the last parts of grammar to be mastered. Mistakes such as those in the exercise on pages 85 and 86 (e.g. numbers 32, 33, 35 and 36) for example are commonplace. For learners who make such mistakes, written exercises and examples need to be given along with constant and consistent correction of spoken errors. In addition, during reading exercises, learners can be asked to highlight examples of the past simple and present perfect tenses i.e. to identify them in context.

Learners also need to be given the opportunity to learn, through practice (speaking and listening, and reading and writing), the simple past and past participles of the most common regular and irregular verbs, which can be found listed in many language textbooks. Naturally, if you're in a position, and you have the time, to record learners' spoken English with a view to providing detailed and constructive feedback to assist their language development, then this should be done.

Below is the transcript of a conversation with a learner in my class, followed by an analysis of the transcribed data and recommendations for developing the learner's language skills. This is followed by an analysis of the learner's reading, and an analysis of a piece of writing submitted by the learner. The learner in question is a 28 year old Polish man, who has been living in Britain for 1 year. He left school at 18, having obtained a place at a nearby university where he studied business studies for 4 years. He gives the impression that he had a relatively comfortable lifestyle in Poland. Nevertheless, he wanted to come to Britain in order to work for more money, and realised that improving his English would help him achieve a better job.

The learner joined the Entry level 2 ESOL conversational English class in January '07 having been initially assessed (in reading and writing) at Entry level 2. The learner comes across as quite confident and will, whether responding to a question from the tutor or from another student in a prepared text, often go 'off script' i.e. add additional words or phrases in order to 'show off' his knowledge. Similarly, he is often one of the first students to contribute an opinion to open class discussions, particularly if the discussion is based around a subject he is interested in (such as sport or Polish customs).

Transcription of Taped Recording between tutor (T) and ESOL learner (L)

1 <T>   Um I know you're from Poland. Which part of Poland are you from again?

2 <L>   I am from uh south west Poland.

3 <T>   OK. Um what's the name of your town?

4 <L>   Um my town names it's uh Swidniza.

5 <T>   Schwid?

6 <L>   Swidniza.

7 <T>   OK. Can you describe your town? Is it a big place small place?

8 <L>   No it's a small town about sixty thousand people

9 <T>   OK. That's great. Um six thousand people so …

10 <L>   Sixty

11 <T>   Sixty thousand people

12 <L>   Sixty thousand people

13 <T>   So it's a small town?

14 <L>   Yes small town

15 <T>   And can you describe it? What's what … what is it like there?

16 <L>   (silence – 2 secs)

17 <T>   What is it like there?

18 <L>   (silence – 6 secs)

19 <T>   Can you describe the town? Tell me about the town?

20 <L>   (silence – 4 secs)

21 <T>   Are the people there friendly?

22 <L>   Yes people is very friendly this is a … a small town

23 <T>   Yeah

24 <L>   And … everybody know everything about the other person

25 <T>   OK, yeah I know the type of place.

26 <L>   This is a beautiful town with a um new city centre rest restaurant

27 <T>   Yeah OK that's great and um are you in the country? Is it in the countryside?

28 <L>	(silence – 5 secs)	
29 <T>	Is it near other towns or is there much country like grass trees outside?	
30 <L>	Yes … (inaudible)	
31 <T>	OK um and have you been back to Poland recently?	
32 <L>	Er the last time I been to Poland er 6, 7 months ago	
33 <T>	OK, that's fine good um and so how long have you been in England for?	
34 <L>	Now I am here er one year	
35 <T>	One year OK good and in Poland … do you have um a good education system there?	
36 <L>	Yes er we have a good education system	
37 <T>	OK that's great and you're … I think you told me before that you're working, so what is your job here?	
38 <L>	Er now I working on the mortgage paper company I am lorry driver	
39 <T>	Yeah, and do you like your job?	
40 <L>	Yes I like	
41 <T>	OK and what sort of hours are you doing?	
42 <L>	Er usually I working er 9 hours a day	
43 <T>	From?	
44 <L>	From half past er five to half past (inaudible (seven?))	
45 <T>	OK that's fine and um sorry and er how long have you been working where you are?	
46 <L>	Here?	
47 <T>	Yes	
48 <L>	Er I working here 11 er months	
49 <T>	OK good and er you … you live in Luton?	
50 <L>	Yes I live in Luton	
51 <T>	OK and do you have any brothers or sisters?	
52 <L>	Yes I have one sister	
53 <T>	OK.	
54 <L>	She's name Evelina	
55 <T>	OK and um is she married?	
56 <L>	Yes I am married	
57 <T>	No is she married?	
58 <L>	Er Evelina?	
59 <T>	Yes	
60 <L>	No she's not married	

61 <T>   OK and I was just about to ask you are you married?

62 <L>   Yes I am married

63 <T>   OK and er how long have you been married for?

64 <L>   Er I am married 6 years

65 <T>   OK great and um sorry going back to your sister I know it's the other way round now you said um does she speak good English?

66 <L>   My sister?

67 <T>   Yes

68 <L>   Yes she very good speak English

70 <T>   OK better than you?

71 <L>   Yes more than me

72 <T>   OK um when you came to you came to England about a year ago what did your friends think about you coming to England?

73 <L>   (silence – 4 secs) I don't know it's (inaudible)

74 <T>   About you coming to England about about you coming to England

75 <L>   Very big surprise for somebody (inaudible)

76 <T>   OK

77 <L>   Somebody uh going better better life Poland (inaudible)

78 <T>   Yeah that's fine OK good and um OK and what what did you use to do in Poland?

79 <L>   The last my job in Poland uh managing director

80 <T>   Managing director?

81 <L>   Yes

82 <T>   Yeah

83 <L>   Um I recruit people training people and planning media relation

84 <T>   Managing?

85 <L>   Uh media relation

86 <T>   OK media relation

87 <L>   Yes media relation

88 <T>   OK and was that a worthwhile job?

89 <L>   Sorry

90 <T>   Was that a worthwhile job?

91 <L>   (silence – 3 secs)

92 <T>   Um was that did you was that a good job?

93 <L>   Yes very good job

94 <T>   OK and um now you're working in England what kind of work would you like to do if you had the choice (pause) here?

95 <L>   Well if I have if I have the choice

96 \<T> Yeah

97 \<L> I would like to do the same work in Poland

98 \<T> OK

99 \<L> But you know I must learn English

100 \<T> Yeah OK good and um what do you do in your spare time here? What do you do in your spare time?

101 \<L> Spare time?

102 \<T> Your free time here?

103 \<L> I spend my time with my family at home and my wife we going to the park uh we giving food for bird

104 \<T> For?

105 \<L> Bird bird

106 \<T> OK yeah yeah good yeah yeah yeah

107 \<L> (inaudible)

108 \<T> OK do you travel around have you travelled around England much?

109 \<L> Yes uh everyday I travel around England

110 \<T> Yeah

111 \<L> Cos everyday I I making about three four hundred miles

112 \<T> OK (pause) everyday?

113 \<L> Yeah

114 \<T> Yeah OK so where where do you travel to in England? All all everywhere?

115 \<L> Usually I going to Essex

116 \<T> Yeah

117 \<L> Lincolnshire

118 \<T> Yeah

119 \<L> North Northampton Buckinghamshire Hertfordshire and London

120 \<T> So you know the M1 very well

121 \<L> Yeah (laughing)

122 \<T> And and the A1 maybe

123 \<L> (inaudible) M1 very well

124 \<T> Yeah OK

125 \<L> Specially after all (inaudible)

126 \<T> OK and do you like cooking?

127 \<L> Yes I I like cooking

128 \<T> And what's your favourite?

129 \<L> I cooking very well

130 \<T> Yeah OK and what's your favourite dish?

131 \<L> Umm my favourite it's er spaghetti

132 \<T> Yeah yeah yeah

133 \<L> Spaghetti bolognaise

134 \<T> OK yeah good and do you prefer Polish or English food?

135 \<L> Polish (pause) Polish

136 \<T> And um do you like listening to music?

137 \<L> Yes I like listening to music

138 \<T> And what sort of music do you like?

139 \<L> I like rhythm and blues especially

140 \<T> Yeah

141 \<L> I like very like er the Rolling Stones

142 \<T> Yeah

143 \<L> And Pink Floyd er Dire Straits and …

144 \<T> So you're you're an old rocker then?

145 \<L> Yeah

146 \<T> (laughing) OK excellent and um do you like wearing fashionable clothes?

147 \<L> (pause) yes yes

148 \<T> OK good um OK and you've been coming to this English class for a while now where where do you normally um sit in the class?

149 \<L> (pause) I normally sit on the back

150 \<T> OK and how do you find the the other people in the class?

151 \<L> (silence – 3 secs)

152 \<T> What do you think about the other people in the class?

153 \<L> What I think?

154 \<T> Yeah

155 \<L> It's very people is very friendly I like these people

156 \<T> OK that's great OK I think that that's good that's excellent … and just one more question Dariusz um when you speak English everyday at work or (inaudible) do English people ever correct you?

157 \<L> No nobody don't correct me

158 \<T> No never?

159 \<L> Never

160 \<T> Apart from me

161 \<L> Yes

162 \<T> (laughing) OK thanks

Analysis of Transcribed Data

Grammar

The learner's native language is Polish, and on the basis that it is a Slavonic language related to Russian (Monk and Burak 1987) and sharing many of its grammatical and phonological features, it will be assumed that references to grammatical or phonological features relating to Russian learners in any text (e.g. the chapter on 'Russian speakers' in Monk and Borak 1987) will also apply to Polish learners.

The learner makes errors in his speech with the use of the present simple tense. For example, on 103, the learner says '… we going to the park' instead of '… we go to the park', on 111 '… I making three four hundred miles' instead of '… I make three four hundred miles' and on 129 'I cooking very well' instead of 'I cook very well'. In the Adult ESOL Core Curriculum (2001), it states (section Lr/E2) that *'Adults should learn to:* respond to requests for information' and in so doing:

> 'recognise questions of the *wh-* type and … recognise verb forms and time markers to understand the time to which a speaker is referring and respond appropriately, e.g. (a) present simple …
>
> **(DfES 2001: 132)**

The learner makes errors in his speech with the use of the present perfect tense. For example, in response to the question (33) ' … how long have you been in England for?' the learner replies (34), ' … I am here … one year' instead of, 'I have been here for one year' and in response to the question (63) '… how long have you been married for?' the learner replies (64) '… I am married for 6 years' instead of 'I have been married for 6 years'. The DfES (2001) states (section Sc/E3) that:

> *'Adults should learn to:* **ask questions to obtain personal or factual information** … in a range of tenses, e.g.: (a) present perfect
>
> **(DfES 2001: 182)**

The learner also makes errors in his speech with the use of the present perfect continuous tense. For example, in response to the question (45) '… how long have you been working where you are?' the learner replies (48) ' … I working here er 11 months' instead of 'I have been working here for 11 months'.

The reasons for the above errors relate to the fact that Slavonic languages have, according to Monk and Borak (1987: 122) 'no present perfect or present progressive forms' and that they have 'only one simple present tense'.

The learner makes errors in his speech with the subject verb agreement. For example, on 22 and 155, the learner says '… people is very friendly…' instead of 'people are very friendly, on 24 '… everybody know everything…' instead of 'everybody knows everything…', and on 68 '… she very good speak English' instead of 'she speaks English very well'. The DfES (2001) states (section Ws/ E3) that:

> *Adults should learn to:* use basic sentence grammar accurately – understand that a verb and its subject must agree …
>
> **(DfES 2001: 240)**

The learner makes errors during the dialogue with the word order of adjectives. For example, on 79 the learner says 'the last my job in Poland' instead of 'my last job in Poland' and on 68, '… she very good speak English' instead of '… she speaks very good English'. The DfES (2001) states (section Ws/E2) that:

> *Adults should learn to:* use appropriate word order in simple and compound sentences, and be aware of how this may differ from word order in their other languages
>
> **(DfES 2001: 158)**

In Polish/Russian, the word order is noun + adjective. The learner makes errors during the dialogue with prepositions. For example, on 38, the learner says, '… I working on the Moorgate Paper Company…' instead of 'I am working for the Moorgate Paper Company' and on 149, 'I normally sit on the back' instead of 'I normally sit at the back'. The learner also makes errors in his speech through the omission of articles. For example, on 24 the learner says 'yes people is very friendly' instead of 'yes the people are very friendly' and on 38, '… I am lorry driver' instead of '… I am a lorry driver'. The DfES (2001) states (section Sc/E2) that:

> *Adults should learn to:* express statements of fact – use with some accuracy grammatical forms suitable for the levels, e.g. (c) prepositions of place and time (d) indefinite and definite article.
>
> **(DfES 2001: 110)**

Monk and Burak (1987: 126) argue that for Slavonic learners, 'The use of prepositions often results in errors'. One of the reasons for the learners difficulties with articles is the fact that there are no articles in the Polish language. As Monk and Burak (1987: 125) state, 'One of the initial problems for … learners is learning how to use articles in general'. However, the learner uses articles correctly in much of the conversation e.g on 8, '… it's a small town …', on 149, ' I normally sit on the back' and on 137, 'I like listening to music'.

The learner makes an error on 71, with the use of the comparative adjective. In responding to the question '… better than you?', referring to whether or not his English was better than his sister's, the learner replies 'yes more than me' instead of 'yes better than me'. Monk and Burak (1987:125) state that Slavonic speakers have 'difficulties … in the formation of the degrees of comparison of the adjectives *bad, good* and *far'*. The DfES (2001: 116) states that *'Adults should learn to: -* be able to make comparisons, using comparative adjectives, both with *–er* and with *more'*

The learner makes errors during the dialogue with the use of deictic markers e.g. whilst talking about his home town in Poland on 22, the learner says '… this is a … a small town' instead of 'it's a small town' and on 155, in response to how he finds the other people in the class, the says ' I like these people' instead of 'I like them'. The DfES (2001: 132) states that *'Adults should learn to:* understand some deictic markers, e.g. this, that, here, there'.

Other grammatical errors include the misuse of the pronoun and misuse of the common rule of the genitive (to express possession i.e. 's) on 54 where the learner says 'she's name Evelina' instead of 'her name is Evelina'.

In order to develop the learner's understanding and correct use of the above verb tenses and grammatical forms, the learner could first be allowed to listen to the recorded conversation and be given the opportunity to correct his mistakes. If the mistakes are not identified (or only partly identified), the learner should then be given the opportunity to read the transcript of the taped recording between tutor and learner, and again be given the chance to identify his own mistakes.

In supporting the learner's literacy development, a range of activities/tasks should be demonstrated by the tutor. In each case, the target language should be presented clearly with the use of appropriate models and the learner given the opportunity to practice through repetition. Krashen (1981: 2) argues that, 'Conscious language learning … is thought to be helped a great deal by error correction and the presentation of explicit rules' and that, 'Error correction … helps the learner come to the correct mental representation of the linguistic generalization'.

In addition, a series of structured written exercises should be given, such as those from Murphy (1997: 18) in order to reinforce the correct use of the relevant tense or grammatical form. These exercises can be supplemented by the DfES's (2003) ESOL Skills for Life materials, which place the learning of the relevant tense or grammatical form into an everyday context through a series of speaking and listening, and writing exercises. In so doing, a variety of learning styles can be taken into consideration.

Discourse Features

Reflecting on the learner's use of language in the transcript, it can be seen that a variety of common discourse features are used including:

Fillers (um, uh etc.) e.g. on 4, '**um** my town … it's **uh** …' and 32, '**er** the last time I been to Poland **er** 6, 7 months ago'

Discourse markers, which according to Carter and McCarthy (1997: 14), 'help speakers to negotiate their way through talk …' e.g. on 95, the learner says '**well** if I have … the choice' and 99, 'but **you know** I must learn English'. Carter and McCarthy (1997: 14) also state that 'In conversation in general phrases such as *you know* … serve to check understanding and to soften and personalise the interactive style …'. Furthermore, the DfES (2001: 112) states that '*Adults should learn to:* give personal information – know and use discourse markers to introduce a response, especially in informal situations, e.g. *well.*'

Deixis, which according to Carter and McCarthy (1997: 13), '… describes what may be termed the orientational features of language' e.g. on 38, the learner says 'er **now** I working …'. Carter and McCarthy (1997: 13) also state that '… words like *now* and *then* relate to the current moment of utterance…'. However, as explained above, the learner also makes errors with the use of deictic markers.

Adverbs e.g. '**usually**' which appears on 42 and 115 and '**normally**' on 149. Carter and McCarthy (1997: 12) state that 'words like … *usually* … are used frequently by speakers to indicate personal attitudes and judgements' and that in so doing, they 'play an important part in … modifying whole propositions'.

Phonological patterns

On 26 and 52, the short vowel sound /ɪ/ in 'c**i**ty' and 's**i**ster' is pronounced more like the long vowel /iː/. On 83 and 85, the long vowel sound /iː/ in m**e**dia is pronounced more like the short vowel /e/. On 103, the long vowel sound /ɜː/ in 'b**ir**d' is pronounced more like the short vowel /ɪ/ followed by the consonant /r/. The reason for the above is because, according to Monk and Barak (1987: 117), one of the main features which distinguishes English from the Slavonic sound system is 'the absence of the short-long vowel differentiation'.

On 38, 42 and 48, the long vowel sound /ɜː/ in 'w**or**king' is pronounced slightly differently. The difficulty for the learner in the pronunciation of this phoneme, is due to the fact that it doesn't have an equivalent sound in slavonic languages (Monk and Barat 1987). The pronunciation is perhaps similar to a vowel in the learner's native language (Polish).

On 3, the learner has difficulty pronouncing the 'th' in 'sou**th**' correctly (the interdental), and likewise with the 'th' in '**th**ousand' on 8. In both cases, the pronunciation tends towards 't'. Monk and Borak (1987: 118) explain that this difficulty is due to the absence of the sound (Theta) in Slavonic languages. On 32 and 48, the learner has difficulty in pronouncing the 'ths' in mon**ths**. In both cases, it sounds like 'mon**ts**'. Monk and Borak (1987: 119) argue that the combination of 'th' and 's' (as in months or clothes) is 'generally a major challenge even for quite good learners, who often tend to substitute /ts/'.

On 50, the learner pronounces the place name 'Luton' incorrectly by pronouncing the vowel 'o' between the 't' and the 'n'. Monk and Burak (1987: 119) point out that Slavonic speakers 'tend to insert the neutral sound /ə/ in the combinations /tl/, /dl/, /tn/…' However, in this case, the learner appears to have inserted the /ɒ/ sound.

In terms of word stress, the learner is, in general, consistent with where he places stress on each word. For example, for high frequency nouns, such as people (22), centre (26) and family (103), and adjectives such as Polish (135) and favourite (131) the learner tends to place stress on the first syllable, and for high frequency verbs such as working (38 and 42) and cooking (127 and 129), the learner tends to place stress on the second syllable. However, in long English place names with suffixes (e.g. Hertfordshire), the suffix (i.e. shire) is not normally stressed. However, on 117, and 119, the learner can clearly be heard placing stress on the suffixes (shire) of the place names Lincolnshire, Buckinghamshire and Hertfordshire.

In terms of sentence stress on 58 (er Evelina?) and 66 (my sister?), the learner uses rising intonation towards the end of each sentence/word to indicate the interrogative. On 8, in responding to the question 'Is it a big place?', (relating to the size of his home town) the learner replies in the negative and places the stress at the beginning of the sentence ('no it's a small town about sixty thousand people'), and the intonation therefore declines. Similarly, on 40 (yes I like), 68 (yes she very good speak English), and 93 (yes very good job) when replying to questions in the affirmative, the learner places the stress at the beginning of each sentence and the intonation declines. In each of the above answers that the learner gives, the intonation/sentence stress occurs as a result of the learner's enthusiasm for the subject matter. In much of the dialogue however, the intonation and sentence stress is fairly consistent.

In terms of sentence rhythm, Monk and Burak (1987: 119) argue that it can present difficulties for learners, and cite the example of how 'learners often pronounce the slower 'strong' forms of words like *as, than, can, must* or *have* instead of the faster 'weak' forms. Listening to the transcript, it is clear that the slower, stronger form of the word 'have' (36 and 52) is pronounced, and likewise with 'than' (72).

Relating to the above, the DfES (2001) states (section Sc/E2) that:

> *Adults should learn to:* **articulate the sounds of English to make meaning understood – distinguish between similar-sounding phonemes, to make meaning clear**
>
> **DfES (2001: 102)**

In addition, it states that:

> *Adults should learn to:* **use stress and intonation adequately to make speech comprehensible and meaning understood – develop awareness that English has a stress-timed rhythm and make a distinction between stressed and unstressed syllables in their own words**
>
> **DfES (2001: 102)**

To that end the DfES (2001: 103) recommends a range of sample activities in order to assist learners with the above, including; listening 'to questions with end-fall or end-rise intonation to identify which are polite and which are not' ; practising 'minimal pair words … drawn from a recipe or a discussion on cooking from different countries'; listening 'to a simplified weather report in order to identify the number of syllables in familiar words'; and working 'on stressing content words appropriately as part of an activity around giving and responding to instructions'.

Analysis of Reading

The learner read from the introduction to Charles Dickens' 'A Tale of Two Cities'. The book is a Penguin reader containing simplified text at an Upper Intermediate level (level 5). The learner has difficulty in pronouncing the 'th' in '**th**ough', with the pronunciation tending more towards /t/. This error is similar to an error he makes in the audio-taped conversation with the 'th' in the word 'thousand'. He also has difficulty in pronouncing the 'th' in 'with', with the pronunciation tending more towards /v/. Both cases are due to the absence of the sound /θ/ in Slavonic languages. The dipthongised /ʊə/ sound in pop**u**lar is pronounced more like the long vowel /uː/. The neutral 'schwa' sound /ə/ in 'Portsm**ou**th' is pronounced more like the diphthong /aʊ/. The long vowel /ɜː/ sound in **ea**rn is pronounced more like the long vowel /iː/. This is due to the fact that the /ɜː/ sound is not found in Slavonic languages. Ironically, the learner mispronounces the 'o' in 'polish', pronouncing it as /əʊ/ rather than /ɒ/. This could be because during parts of the reading, the learner is focussing on one word at a time rather than looking at the context of the sentence.

In general, the learner is correctly able to pronounce words ending in 'ed' e.g. 'helped', 'shaped', 'moved' and 'Determined' i.e. he is able to pronounce the two consonants at the end together. However, with the word 'influenced', the learner pronounces the /e/ sound between the 'c' and the 'd' instead of omitting it and pronouncing the /d/ sound directly after the /s/ sound.

When pronouncing the 'du' in 'education', the learner pronounces /d/ followed by /uː/, but omits the pronunciation of the /j/ sound, which occurs between the two. However, in pronouncing the 'tu' in 'situation', the learner does pronounce the /j/ sound between the two. Monk and Barak (1973) argue that speakers of Slavonic languages have difficulties 'in pronouncing… /d/ … followed by /j/, as in *situation*, *education*… '. However, they also point out that such learners have difficulties with 'the initial clusters /tw/…' and 'pr' although the learner pronounces the words the 'tw' in 'twelve' and the 'pr' in 'prison' correctly.

The learner omits the endings of a couple of words, namely the 'ed' in 'attend**ed**' and the 'ness' in 'hopeless**ness**', and has a lot of difficulty in pronouncing the word 'anxieties'. In each case, the learner could have struggled because of lack of familiarity with the words. The DfES (2001) states that:

> *Adults should learn to*: use a variety of reading strategies to help read and understand an increasing range of unfamiliar words
>
> **DfES (2001: 230)**

The DfES (2001: 231) also suggests some strategies that can be used to achieve this, including; 'visual strategies' where 'words with certain letter patterns' are highlighted; 'structural strategies' where 'words with common suffixes and prefixes in a text' are underlined and their meaning discussed; 'contextual strategies' where 'with guidance, learners use … context to understand' unfamiliar words in a given text and 'the sentence containing the word' and 'phonic strategies' where 'learners identify unfamiliar words, including unfamiliar names, in a narrative'.

It is clear from the way in which the learner reads that he has a good understanding of punctuation. For example he stops at the end of each sentence, and pauses at each comma. This is due to the fact that the learner is literate in his own language, and because, according to Monk and Barak (1987: 121), in Slavonic languages 'punctuation marks and the rules for their use are basically similar to English.'

Writing Sample

The learner was asked to look at the following picture and write a paragraph describing what he could see.

Tower Bridge and HMS Belfast

On the picture we're see Thames River and Tower Bridge.
Tower Bridge was completed in 1894 after 8 years of construction
Tower Bridge is very big strong and beautiful speciall 5 o'clock morning when is dark and lights.
On the picture we're see ships HMS Belfast. I were on the Tower Bridge last week ~~and~~ [] crosing to the south side of London in my lorry

Analysis of Writing Sample

On the first and eighth lines of the written text, the learner writes 'On the picture we've see Thames River/ships HMS Belfast …' instead of 'In the picture we **can** see the Thames River/the ship HMS Belfast'. It is clear that the learner is not familiar with the use of the modal + infinitive i.e. 'can + infinitive'. In addition, the learner makes an error relating to subject-verb agreement in writing, 'I were on the …' instead of 'I **was** on the …'. However, the learner uses the past passive tense correctly when he writes 'Tower Bridge was completed in …'. The DfES (2001: 240) states that: 'An adult will be expected to: use correct basic grammar, e.g. appropriate verb tense, subject-verb agreement' and should 'know that the range/usage of tenses in English does not always correspond directly with the range in learners' other languages, … '. Murphy (1997: 70) offers a range of exercises in order to practice using 'can + infinitive'.

With regard to the use of prepositions, the learner in the above sentences uses 'On' rather than 'In'. In addition the learner writes 'Tower Bridge is … beautiful speciall 5 o'clock morning …' i.e. he omits the preposition 'at' between 'speciall' and '5' and 'in the' between '5 o'clock' and 'morning'. However, he also uses prepositions correctly within the written text e.g. ' … **in** 1894 …', '… crosing **to** the south side **of** London **in** my lorry'. In terms of the use of articles, the learner has, as indicated above, omitted the definite article on two occasions, but has also used it correctly. The reasons for the difficulties that speakers of Slavonic languages have with the use of prepositions and articles, have been outlined above (see analysis of transcribed data – grammar). Murphy (1997) offers a range of exercises in order to practice the use of prepositions and articles.

The learner correctly uses capital letters for proper nouns (e.g. Thames River and HMS Belfast), for the beginning of sentences, and for the pronoun 'I'.

In terms of the learner's spelling, the majority of words in the written text are spelt correctly. However, this could be due to the fact the learner has chosen the words in the written text selectively i.e. has just chosen words that he is familiar with and confident of spelling correctly. The errors that he does make are 'speciall' instead of 'especially' and 'crosing' instead of 'crossing'. The basic and key skill builder communication level 1 workbook 3 for spelling and handwriting (West Nottinghamshire College: 2004) has some clear guidelines (and an exercise) as to how suffixes should be added to verbs, along with a range of other spelling guidelines and accompanying exercises. Workbook 4 contains a range of activities for developing learners' vocabulary. The DfES (2001) suggests a range of strategies for developing learners' spelling and vocabulary, including building up 'word lists of groups of words with common letter patterns and/or sound-symbol associations', 'vocabulary for a particular context', practising 'spelling with gap-fill exercises' and the use of the look – cover – say – write – check method. Where a sound-letter correspondence is being taught, care should be taken to ensure that the learner has an opportunity to hear the sound. Furthermore, when teaching new vocabulary to ESOL learners, the meaning, spoken form of the word and written form of the word should all be emphasised. Writing frames, prepared for a range of levels, can be a useful strategy for developing writing skills in ESOL learners. Examples of writing frames (writing letters, applying for courses etc.) can be found in Spiegel and Sutherland (1999). ESOL learners could also benefit from the support of pictures within the learning materials.). In supporting general English acquisition through the written (and spoken) word, teachers should avoid the danger of overloading the text with unknown words.

On the basis that the learner, as mentioned previously, is generally well educated and literate in his own language, and on the basis that he comes across as a keen and motivated learner, who is currently living and working in the UK and therefore exposed to the English language on a daily basis, the learner is certainly in a position to make improvements in his language and literacy skills (speaking, reading and writing) outlined above.

As mentioned earlier, there are many resources available for developing literacy skills. Likewise, there are many books and resources (some already referred to) available for developing language skills. This book, however, as was also mentioned earlier, is also about providing a framework, and ideas, for developing those skills. Nevertheless, the following resources have been written in order to allow learners the opportunity to practise exercises aimed at developing their speaking, reading and writing skills. The initial reading and writing exercises are provided as examples of ESOL learning assessments which can be used in the context of ascertaining (through the mark scheme) an initial level, or as a learning resource whereby feedback is given focusing on error correction. The first resource for example focuses on common errors made in everyday spoken English by ESOL learners. Naturally the list can be added to. Although the emphasis of the worksheet is on developing fluency of spoken English, it should be used, through error correction, for developing reading and writing skills also, in the context of the development of one skill reinforcing another.

They include examples that, based on my experience with ESOL speakers, offer the last bastions of resistance to grammatical fluency, including the aforementioned difficulties that learners have in differentiating between the correct use of the present perfect and simple past (e.g. numbers 32, 33, 35 and 36), and knowing how to position the verb (including the negative form) following 'wh' questions (e.g. numbers 27, 31, 39 and 41) as well as errors relating to subject verb agreement, the correct use of 'to do' as an auxiliary verb and incorrect use of articles etc. Naturally, depending on the level of the learners in any given group, the errors can be placed together in categories in order to reinforce a particular grammatical rule that has been taught or, as laid out in the exercise, randomly in order to reflect on, and reinforce, several areas together to test learners' memory and help develop overall fluency.

Similarly, the other resources ('Using Prepositions', 'Going to the shops' and

'What do you do in your spare time?') can be used to develop each skill in an integrated context. It should be borne in mind that, as mentioned earlier in the context of developing literacy skills, although the focus of a particular exercise may be on developing an aspect of language, the opportunity can still be taken to address any other issues, whether it be related to pronunciation, grammar or meaning of vocabulary etc. Furthermore, through developing their language skills, ESOL learners should be given the opportunity to develop their literacy skills through, for example, the methods and resources advocated earlier in the book, including the exercises following the discussion-based articles, the punctuation reading exercises, literacy exercises, letter writing exercises (including error corrections), and the Functional Skills reading and writing exercises.

ESOL Learning Assessment: Reading

Read the text below, then answer the questions that follow:

Have you joined the Organ Donor Register?

Organ donation is giving an organ to help someone who needs a transplant. Kidneys, heart, liver, lungs, pancreas and the small bowel can all be transplanted. Transplants are one of the biggest achievements of modern medicine and can save or greatly enhance the lives of seriously ill patients. However, they depend completely on donors and their families consenting to organ donation.

Research shows that 96% of us would take an organ if we needed one. However, only 29% of us have taken action and joined the NHS Organ Donor Register

If you believe in organ donation, prove it.

The NHS Organ Donor Register gives hope to more than 10,000 people of all ages across the UK who need an organ transplant. However, many people, on average three a day, die before they can have a transplant because there are simply not enough organs available.

Do you believe in organ donation? If you would take an organ, would you be willing to give one and help someone live after your death? Register now!

How to register?

It's simple to join the NHS Organ Donor Register using one of the following methods:

- Go to www.organdonation.nhs.uk
- Call 0300 123 23 23
- Text SAVE to 84118
- Complete and post **this leaflet**

Please register my details on the NHS Organ Donor Register

Please complete in CAPITAL LETTERS using a black ballpoint pen.

* indicates that a field must be completed

My name and address

Suname* _____

Forename(s)* _____

Date of birth* _____ / _____ / _____   Male ☐* Female ☐*

Address* _____

_____

_____

_____ Postcode* _____

Telephone _____

Mobile _____

Email _____

My wishes

I want to donate: (Please tick the boxes that apply)

A. any of my organs and tissue ☐ or

B. my kidneys ☐   heart ☐   liver ☐   small bowel ☐

    eyes ☐   lungs ☐   pancreas ☐   tissue ☐

for transplantation after my death.

Signature: _____

Date: _____

My ethnic origin

There's a better chance of getting a closer match and a successful transplant if the donor and recipient are from the same ethnic group. Please tick the ethnic group which best describes you.

White: British ☐ Irish ☐ Other ☐

Mixed: White/Black Caribbean ☐ White/Asian ☐

Asian or Asian British: Indian ☐ Pakistani ☐ Bangladeshi ☐ Other ☐

Black or Black British: Caribbean ☐ African ☐ Other ☐

Other ethnic categories: Chinese ☐ Other ☐

Not stated: ☐

Data Protection Assurance. Completion of this form is for the purpose of recording your wishes to become an organ donor. All information provided to NHS Blood and Transplant is used in accordance with the Data Protection Act 1998.

If you wish to amend or withdraw your record from the NHS Organ Donor Register, you can do so by calling the Organ Donor Line on 0300 123 23 23, visiting www.organdonation.nhs.uk or writing to us at the address overleaf.

NHS Organ Donor Register

The NHS Organ Donor Register records the details of people who have registered their wishes to be an organ and/or tissue donor after their death.

This confidential information is used by authorised medical staff to establish whether a person wanted to donate.

Anyone can register. Age isn't a barrier to becoming an organ or tissue donor; people in their 70s and 80s have become donors and saved many lives. Most medical conditions don't rule you out either.

One donor can save or transform up to nine lives. It is only through the generosity of people like you that lives can be saved.

Register now

Please let those closest to you know your wishes about organ donation.

Question 1

What is the main purpose of the article? Circle a, b, c or d:

a) to inform you about something
b) to complain about something
c) to give an opinion about something
d) to persuade you about something (2 marks)

Question 2

On which line has a question mark been incorrectly used?

_____ (1 mark)

Question 3

Look at the section under 'NHS Organ Donor Register.' Which word means *official*?

_____

Under the same section, which word means *kindness*?

_____

Under the same section, which word means *private*?

_____

Under the same section, which word means to give *voluntarily*?

_____

Under the same section, which word means *change*?

_____

Look at the section under 'Have you joined the Organ Donor Register?' Which word means *improve*?

_____

Under the same section, which word means *agreeing*?

_____

Under the same section, which word means *intestines*?

_____

Look at the section under 'Data Protection Assurance.' Which word means *alter*?

_____

Look at the section under 'If you believe in organ donation, prove it.' Which word means *prepared*?

_____

Look at the section under 'My ethnic origin.' Which word means beneficiary?

_____

(11 marks)

Question 4

Which of the following are **not** required in order to register as an organ donor?
a) Date of birth   b) Postcode   c) Forename   d) Telephone number   e) Address

(2 marks)

Question 5

Which of the following would you need to do in order to alter your record from the NHS Organ Donor Register?

     a) Text SAVE to 84118
     b) Go to www.organregistration.nhs.uk
     c) Phone 0300 123 23 23
     d) Send an email to organdonation.nhs.uk   (2 marks)

Question 6

How must the name and address on the NHS Organ Donor Register be completed?

_____

(2 marks)

ESOL Learning Assessment: Writing

Look at the two pictures above, chose one and write 5 sentences about what you see:

1. _____

   _____

2. _____

   _____

3. _____

   _____

4. _____

_____

5. _____

_____

(10 marks)

On the lines below, write a short text about yourself (between 100 and 150 words). You could write about your family, your interests, the country you are from, your education and your work experience:

_____

_____

_____

_____

_____

_____

_____

_____

_____

_____

_____

_____

_____

_____

_____

_____

_____

_____ (10 marks)

ESOL Exercise

Choose and underline the correct form of the verb:

1. Daffodils (grow / are growing) in spring.
2. We (knew / have known) him for 5 years.
3. Jack called while I (worked / was working) on my presentation.
4. Would you like a sandwich? No, thanks, I (have already eaten / ate).

5. Where is Rosie? She (waters / is watering) the plants in the back garden.

6. I cut my finger while I (cooked / was cooking) dinner last night.

7. This is the most beautiful house I (have ever seen / ever saw).

8. Wait for me! I (am coming / come now).

9. I (have not watched / did not watch) 'Gladiator' yet.

10. We (lived / have lived) here since 1998.

Correcting mistakes made in everyday spoken English by ESOL learners

The following sentences contain common errors made in everyday spoken English by ESOL learners. Find the error in each of the following sentences.

1.   What does you do for a living? _____

2.   I'm teacher in a primary school. _____

3.   Do you like you job? _____

4.   Does she likes her job? _____

5.   She no like him. _____

    Why she no like him? _____

6.   He don't go to the maths class very often. _____

7.   We went to nice restaurant last night. _____

8.   Did you saw that film yesterday? _____

9.   Does he has enough money for his train fare? _____

10. I going to London this weekend. _____

11. They don't married yet. _____

12. I did told you about the game didn't I? _____

13. Did you enjoy the film? Yes, I liked. _____

14. What do a mechanic do? A mechanic mends cars.

    _____

15. What do journalists do? A journalists write for newspapers.

    _____

16. What does a nurse do? A nurse look after people in hospital.

    _____

17. Do he go out last night? _____

18. Do you going out later? _____

19. I think he's goes out later on. _____

20. Is he a guy you saw in the pub earlier? _____

21. When you go to the shop, can you get me the pint of milk and a loaf of bread? _____

22. Did you asked him about his new job? _____

23. I've made too much mistakes in this test. _____

24. I have 24 years old. _____

25. The people here is very friendly. _____

26. Everybody know about their problems. _____

27. When you will teach me about English grammar?_____

28. Do you know what the solution are?_____

29. Those area are quite dangerous._____

30. They haven't announce the train's departure time yet._____

31. Why he won't do his homework?_____

32. My mother has visited, but my father didn't come yet._____

33. I didn't go there yet._____

34. Why we have to change our Government?_____

35. I have worked with children at a school a few years ago._____

36. I have been to London yesterday._____

37. They helped them by take the heavier items in the truck._____

38. There were less people at the station than usual for a Monday morning.

   _____

39. Why you didn't go to the meeting last night?_____

40. The kids fought and play together until it was their bedtime._____

41. Who you are supporting in tonight's game? _____

42. Was you at the match yesterday?_____

43. Do you usually watched Eastenders?_____

44. There were less noise than usual._____

45. His brother felt that he already done enough._____

46. If I could afford it, I will go to China again this year._____

47. We knew that we shouldn't off run on the grass._____

48. She refused to borrow him her copy of the exam paper._____

49. Who you think will win the game?_____

50. Why you don't come to the class more often? _____

51. How he managed to ran up such a high bill, I'll never know!_____

52. The dog tried hard to took back his bone._____

53. There's many articles in the newspaper._____

54. He was able to get the gist off the story._____

55. When you get to your destination, can you sent me a postcard?_____

56. They fought hard and win, but it was a pyrrhic victory._____

57. She fall down, but managed to get up quickly._____

58. How long have you know him?_____

59. He had few than 50 art-works left in his collection._____

60. His directions wasn't as accurate as they could have been._____

61. What they must do to achieve their goal?_____

62. Why did you waiting for so long?_____

63. How you feel about losing your job?_____

64. Paul used walk to work every day._____

65. What time does Sally normally goes to playgroup?_____

66. Brian still walk to work every day._____

67. Why you're taking so long?_____

68. They couldn't of known what was going to happen._____

69. I took my friend's dog for walk in the countryside._____

70. John tried to taken the biscuit out of Kat's mouth._____

71. I hear it on the radio this morning._____

72. I done a lot of housework today._____

73. You must to be on time for your lessons._____

74. She didn't listened to a single word I said._____

75. Have you met me mother yet?_____

76. The rain coming, so go inside!_____

77. We couldn't see no changes in him at all._____

78. When is George go home?_____

79. I can't let you to make such a big mistake._____

80. This is the most great house I've ever seen._____

81. I will call you when I will get there._____

82. It's more worse than I thought it would be._____

83. There were less people there than I thought there
    would be._____

84. If you will go to town, will you get me a takeaway?_____

85. How many more time do they need to be told?_____

86. She went straight to home after the concert had finished._____

87. James weren't really supposed to tell his students._____

88. It'll be more better if you tell him yourself._____

89. There are much more crime in cities now than
there used to be._____

90. The internet is so faster than it used to be. _____

91. At the end of the shift, there are still six students left in
the waiting room._____

92. The drivers couldn't understood why they had to
wait so long._____

93. The childrens were playing happily in the courtyard._____

94. How many actress does it take to change a light-bulb?_____

95. A noisy noises annoys an oyster!_____

96. The writer was clearly gets bored at this stage._____

97. The box of wine were stacked up in the kitchen._____

98. Ahmed run as fast as he could to get to the match on time._____

99. His sister advised him to practise every nights._____

100. The football manager was force to resign from his job._____

101. I object to the Dalmatians be put into room 101!_____

102. He's made it clear about his position last week._____

103. He went yesterday to his friend's house._____

104. Michael and James picked put their costumes
swimming in the bag._____

105. Usain Bolt is currently the most fastest man on earth._____

106. Helen was a smarter student than most people think._____

107. How do you thinks she feels after not getting the job?_____

108. At the end of a long night, there was only 3 people left
in the competition._____

109. "It's been hard, day's night and I've been working
like a dog" he sang._____

110. This is last sentence that you have to correct,
so I'll make it an easy one._____

Correcting mistakes made in everyday spoken English by ESOL learners (answers)

1. What **do** you do for a living?
2. I'm **a** teacher in a primary school.
3. Do you like **your** job?
4. Does she **like** her job?
5. She **doesn't** like him. Why **doesn't** she like him?
6. He **doesn't** go to the maths class very often.
7. We went to **a** nice restaurant last night.
8. Did you **see** that film yesterday?
9. Does he **have** enough money for his train fare?
10. **I'm** going to London this weekend.
11. They **aren't** married yet.
12. I did **tell** you about the game didn't I?
13. Did you like the film? Yes, I **did.**
14. What **does** a mechanic do? A mechanic mends cars.
15. What do journalists do? **Journalists** write for newspapers.
16. What does a nurse do? A nurse **looks** after people in hospital.
17. **Did** he go out last night?
18. **Are** you going out later?
19. I think he's **going** out later on.
20. Is he **the** guy you saw in the pub earlier?
21. When you go to the shop, can you get me **a** pint of milk and a loaf of bread.
22. Did you **ask** him about his new job?
23. I've made too **many** mistakes in this test.
24. I **am** 24 years old.
25. The people here **are** very friendly.
26. Everybody **knows** about their problems.
27. When **will you** teach me about English grammar?
28. Do you know what the **solutions** are? *Or* Do you know what the solution **is**?
29. Those **areas** are quite dangerous.
30. They haven't announce**d** the train's departure time yet.

31. Why **won't he** do his homework?

32. My mother has visited, but my father **hasn't** come yet.

33. I **haven't been** there yet.

34. Why **do** we have to change our Government?

35. I **worked** with children at a school a few years ago.

36. I **went** to London yesterday.

37. They helped them by **taking** the heavier items in the truck.

38. There were **fewer** people at the station than usual for a Monday morning.

39. Why **didn't you** go to the meeting last night?

40. The kids fought and **played** together until it was their bedtime.

41. Who **are you** supporting in tonight's game?

42. **Were** you at the match yesterday?

43. Do you usually **watch** Eastenders?

44. There **was** less noise than usual.

45. His brother felt that **he'd** already done enough.

46. If I could afford it, I **would** go to China again this year.

47. We knew that we shouldn't **have** run on the grass.

48. She refused to **lend** him her copy of the exam paper.

49. Who **do** you think will win the game?

50. Why **don't you** come to the class more often?

51. How he managed to **run** up such a high bill, I'll never know!

52. The dog tried hard to **take** back his bone.

53. There **are** many articles in the newspaper.

54. He was able to get the gist **of** the story.

55. When you get to your destination, can you **send** me a postcard?

56. They fought hard and **won**, but it was a pyrrhic victory.

57. She **fell** down, but managed to get up quickly.

58. How long have you **known** him?

59. He had **less** than 50 art-works left in his collection.

60. His directions **weren't** as accurate as they could have been.

61. What **must they** do to achieve their goal?

62. Why did you wait for so long?

63. How **do** you feel about losing your job?

64. Paul used **to** walk to work every day.

65. What time does Sally normally **go** to playgroup?

66. Brian still **walks** to work every day.

67. Why **are you** taking so long?

68. They couldn't **have** known what was going to happen.

69. I took my friend's dog for **a** walk in the countryside.

70. John tried to **take** the biscuit out of Kat's mouth.

71. I **heard** it on the radio this morning.

72. I **did** a lot of housework today.

73. You must be on time for your lessons.

74. She didn't **listen** to a single word I said.

75. Have you met **my** mother yet?

76. The **rain's** coming, so go inside!

77. We couldn't see **any** changes in him at all.

78. When is George **going** home?

79. I can't let you make such a big mistake.

80. This is the **greatest** house I've ever seen.

81. I will call you when I get there.

82. It's worse than I thought it would be.

83. There were **fewer** people there than I thought there would be.

84. If you go to town, will you get me a takeaway?

85. How many more **times** do they need to be told?

86. She went straight home after the concert had finished.

87. James **wasn't** really supposed to tell his students.

88. It'll be **much** better if you tell him yourself.

89. There **is** much more crime in cities now than there used to be.

90. The internet is so **much** faster than it used to be.

91. At the end of the shift, there **were** still six students left in the waiting room.

92. The drivers couldn't **understand** why they had to wait so long.

93. The **children** were playing happily in the courtyard.

94. How many **actresses** does it take to change a light-bulb?

95. A noisy **noise** annoys an oyster!

96. The writer was clearly **getting** bored at this stage.

97. The **boxes** of wine were stacked up in the kitchen.

98. Ahmed **ran** as fast as he could to get to the match on time.

99. His sister advised him to practise every **night**.

100. The football manager was **forced** to resign from his job.

101. I object to the Dalmatians **being** put into room 101!

102. He made it clear about his position last week.

103. He went to his friend's house **yesterday**.

104. Michael and James picked put their **swimming costumes** in the bag.

105. Usain Bolt is currently the fastest man on earth.

106. Helen was a smarter student than most people **thought**.

107. How do you **think** she feels after not getting the job?

108. At the end of a long night, there **were** only 3 people left in the competition.

109. "It's been **a** hard, day's night and I've been working like a dog" he sang.

110. This is **the** last sentence that you have to correct, so I'll make it an easy one.

Using Prepositions

Vocabulary (nouns):

ceiling, clock, dustbin, blue cup, blinds, Kevin's wallet, newspaper, TV, register, electric socket, black bag, textbooks, radiator, cupboard, calculator, teacher's desk, posters, CD player, black corduroy jacket

Prepositions:

in front of, behind, opposite, in, on, next to, on top of, under, over, between

Task 1: Working in pairs, and using the vocabulary and prepositions above, take it in turns to ask where objects are in the room.

Example:

Where's the clock?   It's on the wall.

Where are the textbooks?   The textbooks are on the cupboard.

Task 2: Think of three other objects in the room (not written above). Write three questions below, then pass them to a colleague.

Question 1: ....

Answer: ....

Question 2: ....

Answer: ....

Question 3: ....

Answer: ....

Extension activity

Think of another two objects in the room. Write two more questions below, then pass them on to a colleague.

Question 4: ....

Answer: ....

Question 5: ....

Answer: ....

My English class

© Kevin Norley

Back row: Monika, Magda, Eduardo, Mushtaq, Georgina, Michael
Front row: Raymond, Alice, Agnieszka, Angelina

Using the following prepositions, write sentences about who is where on the lines below:

In between   to the left of   to the right of   next to
in front of   behind   at the end of

For example:

Georgina is standing in between Mushtaq and Michael, and behind Agnieszka.

Raymond is sitting at the end of the front row, to the right of Alice and in front of Magda.

Mushtaq is _____

_____

Eduardo is _____

_____

Magda is _____

_____

Monika is _____

_____

Michael is _____

_____

Alice is _____

_____

Agnieszka is _____

_____

Angelina is _____

_____

Going to the shops

Vocabulary: Supermarket
some vegetables (carrots and broccoli)
a cabbage and a cauliflower
some bananas
a tin of soup
some washing up liquid
some washing powder
some toilet paper
a bunch of flowers
some coffee
a bag of sugar
a pint of milk
some tomatoes
some potatoes or rice
a loaf of bread

Clothes shop
a shirt
a pair of smart trousers
three T-shirts
a pair of jeans
a pair of shoes
a couple of ties
a black jacket
two pairs of socks
a jumper or a sweater
a dress
a skirt
a raincoat
a warm coat for the winter
an umbrella

The Chemist
a small box of paracetamol
some toothpaste
a bar of soap
some cough mixture
a box of multivitamins
a bottle of shampoo

The Newsagent's
a newspaper (the daily mail or
    the independent)
a packet of crisps
a can of pepsi or sprite
a bar of chocolate
a box of chocolates
a couple of pens

Speaking exercise

Using the vocabulary above, and working in pairs, take it in turns to be A and B.
When you are B, choose at least 3 items (things) from the list.

A. Hi .... , I'm going to **Tesco's/ Sainsbury's/
Matalan/ the supermarket/ the chemists/ the newsagents** to
do some shopping**.**
Would you like/ Do you want anything?

B. Yes please, **Can you get me/ I'd like**

.... , ... ,
oh! and ....

Writing exercise

Think of some more items (things) you could buy at the shops above and
write them below.

e.g. a large bottle of water, a dictionary, some fruit juice

....

....

....

....

Extension exercise

In pairs, use some of the items you have listed in the speaking exercise above.

What do you do in your spare time?

I play cricket

I tidy the house

What do you **do** in your spare time?

I cook

Speaking Exercise (In Pairs)

A) Hello, I'm .... , what's your name?

B) My name's ....

A) Where are you from?

B) I'm from ....

A) What do you **do** in your spare time?

B) I ....

A) What else do you do in your spare time?

B) I ....

Look at the pictures above.

Picture **1** – What does he do in his spare time? ....

Picture **2** – What does she do in her spare time? ....

What do you like doing in your spare time?

I like playing cricket

I like tidying the house

What do you **like doing** in your spare time?

I like cooking

Speaking Exercise (In Pairs)

A) Hello, I'm .... , what's your name?

B) My name's ....

A) Where are you from?

B) I'm from ....

A) What do you like doing in your spare time?

B) I like ....

A) What else do you like doing in your spare time?

B) I like ....

Think again about what you like doing in your spare time. Working in pairs, also talk about things that you **don't** like doing in your spare time.

For example:

A) What do you like doing in your spare time?

B) I like playing football and watching TV, but I don't like jogging or going to the gym.

A) What do you like doing in your spare time?

B) I like .... and .... ,

but I don't like .... or ....

Phonetic Symbols

Vowels	Examples	Consonants	Examples
ʌ	c<u>u</u>p, l<u>u</u>ck	b	<u>b</u>ad, la<u>b</u>
ɑː	<u>ar</u>m, f<u>a</u>ther	d	<u>d</u>id, la<u>d</u>y
æ	c<u>a</u>t, bl<u>a</u>ck	f	i<u>f</u>, <u>f</u>ind
e	m<u>e</u>t, b<u>e</u>d	g	<u>g</u>ive, fla<u>g</u>
ə	cinem<u>a</u>, <u>a</u>way	h	<u>h</u>ow, <u>h</u>ello
ɜː	l<u>ear</u>n, t<u>ur</u>n	j	<u>y</u>es, <u>y</u>ellow
ɪ	s<u>i</u>tting, h<u>i</u>t	k	<u>c</u>at, ba<u>ck</u>
iː	s<u>ee</u>, h<u>ea</u>t	l	<u>l</u>eg, <u>l</u>ittle
ɒ	h<u>o</u>t, r<u>o</u>ck	m	<u>m</u>an, le<u>m</u>on
ɔː	c<u>a</u>ll, f<u>our</u>	n	<u>n</u>o, te<u>n</u>
ʊ	p<u>u</u>t, c<u>ou</u>ld	ŋ	si<u>ng</u>, fi<u>ng</u>er
uː	f<u>oo</u>d, bl<u>ue</u>	p	<u>p</u>et, ma<u>p</u>
aɪ	m<u>i</u>nd, <u>eye</u>	r	<u>r</u>ed, t<u>r</u>y
aʊ	n<u>ow</u>, <u>ou</u>t	s	<u>s</u>un, mi<u>ss</u>
eɪ	s<u>ay</u>, <u>eigh</u>t	ʃ	<u>sh</u>e, cra<u>sh</u>
oʊ	h<u>o</u>me, g<u>o</u>	t	<u>t</u>ea, ge<u>tt</u>ing
ɔɪ	j<u>oi</u>n, b<u>oy</u>	tʃ	<u>ch</u>eck, <u>ch</u>ur<u>ch</u>
eə	<u>air</u>, wh<u>ere</u>	θ	<u>th</u>ink, bo<u>th</u>
ɪə	n<u>ear</u>, h<u>ere</u>	ð	<u>th</u>is, mo<u>th</u>er
ʊə	p<u>ure</u>, mat<u>ure</u>	v	<u>v</u>oice, fi<u>v</u>e
		w	<u>w</u>et, <u>w</u>ind
		z	<u>z</u>oo, la<u>z</u>y
		ʒ	Plea<u>s</u>ure, vi<u>s</u>ion
		dʒ	<u>j</u>ust, lar<u>ge</u>

References

Bernstein B (1964) *Elaborated and Restricted codes: Their Origins and Some Consequences,* American Anthropologist Monography issue, Ethnology and Speech.

Brown M (May 14th, 2008) in the Sunday Telegraph

Cameron D (1995) *Verbal Hygiene*, London: Routledge

Carter R, McCarthy M (1997) *Exploring Spoken English*, Cambridge: Cambridge University Press

CBI (2006) *Working on the 3 Rs*, London: DfES

Clark L (Jan 2nd, 2009) in 'The Daily Mail', p1

Department for Education and Skills (2001) *Adult ESOL Core Curriculum*, London: DfES.

Department for Education and Skills (2001) *Adult Literacy Core Curriculum*, London: DfES.

Department for Education and Skills (2003) *Skills for Life, Teacher Reference File*

Devine J, Carrell PL, Eskey DE (1987) *Research in English as a second language,* Teachers of English to Speakers of Other Languages: Washington DC

Entwhistle H (1978) *Class, Culture and Education,* London: Methuen.

Gagne R (1985) *The Conditions of Learning*, New York: Holt, Rinehart & Winston

Gardiner A (2003) *English Language (A-Level Study Guide)*, Harlow: Pearson Education Limited

Harmer J (1991) *The Practice of English Language Teaching*, Harlow: Longman

Honey J (1997) *Language is Power*, London: Faber and Faber Limited

Hughes A, Trudgill P (1979) *English Accents and Dialects,* London: Edward Arnold Ltd.

Knowles M (1998) *The Adult Learner*, Houston Texas: Gulf Publishing Company

Kramsch C (1998) *Language and Culture*, Oxford: Oxford University Press

Krashen S (1981) *Second Language Acquisition and Second Language Learning*, Oxford: Pergamon Press

Monk B and Burak A (1987) "Russian speakers" in Swan M and Smith B (Eds) *Learner English*, Cambridge: Cambridge University Press

Murphy R (1997) *Essential Grammar in Use*, Cambridge: Cambridge University Press

Richards J and Rodgers T (2001) *Approaches and Methods in Language Teaching*, Cambridge: Cambridge University Press

Smithers R (2006) in *The Guardian*, p1

Spiegel M, Sutherland H (1999) *Writing Works*, London: London South Bank University

Trudgill P (1994) *Dialects*, London: Routledge Limited

Ur P (1984) *Teaching Listening Comprehension*, Cambridge: Cambridge University Press.

Wallace C (1988) *Learning to read in a multicultural society: the social context of second language literacy,* Hemel Hempstead: Prentice Hall

Woodward F (2012) *Phonics Resources For Older Learners*, Ewell: Imprimata

Zera A, Jupp D (2000) 'Widening Participation' in Smithers A, Robinson P (Eds) *Further Education Reformed*, London: Falmer Press pp 129–140

Online References

Some of the articles used in this book have been based on material from various websites. Where copyright exists, the copyright holders have been attributed alongside the relevant article. The following web pages have been used to source additional reference material:

http://en.wikipedia.org/wiki/Camel
http://en.wikipedia.org/wiki/Wind_power
http://en.wikipedia.org/wiki/Solar_power

Acknowledgements

Permission has been requested to reproduce the following articles:

The more you have in a class, the harder the teacher's job is and *Obese adding to climate crisis - The Guardian*, April 20th, 2009.

One in five school leavers can't read - The Daily Mail, July 19th, 2010.

Cigarettes, diet, alcohol and obesity behind more than 100,000 cancers - Cancer Research UK, press release, Wednesday 7 December 2011

Childhood Obesity - taken from *www.weightlossresources.co.uk*